A Road Map to Education

The CRE-ACT Way

Dorothy Prokes

UNIVERSITY PRESS OF AMERICA,® INC.

Lanham • Boulder • New York • Toronto • Plymouth, UK

Copyright © 2009 by
Dorothy Prokes

University Press of America,® Inc.
4501 Forbes Boulevard
Suite 200
Lanham, Maryland 20706
UPA Acquisitions Department (301) 459-3366

Estover Road
Plymouth PL6 7PY
United Kingdom

Library of Congress Control Number: 2009922310
ISBN: 978-0-7618-4381-8 (paperback : alk. paper)
eISBN: 978-0-7618-4382-5

Cover image by Sister Mary Roberta Connors

∞™ The paper used in this publication meets the minimum
requirements of American National Standard for Information
Sciences—Permanence of Paper for Printed Library Materials,
ANSI Z39.48—1984

To those who
Serve,
Support,
And encourage---
Are willing to "let go" the moment and
venture forth,
Taking chances,
Making changes,
Shaping our todays and tomorrows for
the better, the greater good
of all.

The author

Contents

SECTION 3. THE PERFORMANCE

SECTION 4. IMPLCATIONS FOR THE FUTURE

Preface

"Two roads diverged in a wood, and I,
I took the one less traveled by,
And that has made all the difference."[1]

Robert Frost, *The Road Not Taken*

It is this difference that I want to share with you, a difference that developed from pursuing a creative rather than a traditionally focused approach to education.

During 24 years of working in established school systems at both the elementary and secondary levels, I experienced a growing frustration with my inability to provide for the individual uniqueness of many of the students. A method that worked for one was often very inadequate for others. General standards and procedures formulated by state and national auspices took precedence, and all students were expected to meet them.

It was during my years as a high school English teacher that the CRE-ACT concept shared in this text surfaced within me. My responsibilities included the Speech and Drama Competitions and the All School Play. It was while directing Lerner and Loewe's *PAINT YOUR WAGON* in Breda, Iowa, that I was awakened to the root principle of creative education: each person has to be challenged to "paint" one's own self-becoming image; i.e., "paint" one's own wagon. CREative ACTing became the medium for implementing this transformation. In the process of "painting" with others, each student was filled with life and energy: strengthened and animated as they were invigorated by the others. Once they became involved and took on a dramatic role, there was a change in their very being that did not happen through conventional curricular activities. There was a unique bursting forth of personhood coupled with a determination to "hit the road" and move on into new horizons. Echoing in my mind also was the challenge of John Gardner: "The pressing need today is to educate for an accelerating rate of change. Change is so swift that the latest thing today may be old-fashioned by the time young people enter adulthood, so they must be taught in such a way that they can learn for themselves the new things of tomorrow."[2]

Insights such as these provided the bases for my doctoral research at New York University. If drama had this potential to evoke such growth, it should be given a position in the curricular development of education where its efficacy could be utilized. In my mind, education and theatre had to "cross," to complement each other—a position in which each entity keeps its own identity and enhances the position of the other. It was in that context of doctoral study that CRE-ACTwas born.

This text shares in detail the methodology and paradoxes underlying the CREative ACTing approach. It is an authentic research-tested method of instruction applicable to persons of all ages and cultures, regardless of individual uniqueness.

Most texts present Creative Dramatics as a content subject and provide curricular lessons that are the same for all participants regardless of individual differences or abilities. This text presents Creative Dramatics as a method of instruction concerned primarily with personal development and does not presuppose or rely on dramatic aptitude.

Essentially the role of CREative ACTing is to prepare the participant to employ and apply acquired knowledge spontaneously in a manner that will best meet the demands and needs of a rapidly evolving society. Improvisation is at the heart of the approach. "It is not the world we see that is, in the end, important. What is significant is the world we build out of what we see," Paul Brandwein reminds us.[3] It is the way we perceive that world, how we CRE-ACT with others,what we are able to do with our "self-wagon" that matters. Nothing is alive to us, unless it is vitalized when we "hit the road"—when we act it. Then it becomes part of our inner selves.

Through the encounter of a fresh look and through experiencing things differently in the body we can replace old perceptions with new ones. The refusal to take things for granted is the beginning of a creative response. As we begin to search for ways to bring order out of the disorder we see, we open the way for changing the world around us. It means, with all due respect for a pre-existing Universalizing Order, that we take what we see and know, and put it together in a new way that makes sense and that works.

Teilhard de Chardin reminds us that, "We are collaborators in creation. What you and I are becoming is what the world is becoming."[4]

Are you satisfied with the impact you are making?

NOTES

1. Frost, "The Road Not Taken", Mountain Interval, 1920, http//www.bartleby.com/119/1.html (14 Oct. 2007).

2. Gardner, John, "Your Child's Intelligences" *Scholastic Parent and Child* (Spring, 1996), 11.

3. Brandwein, P. F., *The Permanent Agenda of Man: The Humanities* (New York: Harcourt, Brace, Jovanovich, 1971), 6.

4. Chardin, Teilard de, "Creativity, Use It," *Christopher News Notes* #233 (April 1978), 6.

Acknowledgments

The author wishes to acknowledge her former students who inspired her to listen to their authentic needs and ambitions, taught her how to be creative, and to dream; her religious community, The Franciscan Sisters of the Eucharist, who encouraged and supported her in pursuing the study, research, and establishment of the CREative ACTing approach to education; the chairman and staff of the School of Educational Theatre at New York University who supervised, affirmed, and endorsed the research for establishing the CREative ACTing program; the Franciscan Family Life Center in Pocatello, Idaho, who assisted in establishing the exemplar, The Franciscan CRE-ACT School, and continues to hold it into its future; the parents of the students, and the local Pocatello community for their untiring, active, participation in The Franciscan CRE-ACT School's efforts to achieve its goals and objectives.

In particular, she wishes to thank those directly related to the publication of this text as consultants: Sister Barbara Cline, F.S.E., Mrs. Lenka Peterson, Mrs. Adrianne Adderly, Sister Timothy Prokes, F.S.E., Sister Therese Gutting, F.S.E.; as editorial assistant: Sister Mary Richard Boo, O.S.B.; as technicians: Sister Mary Matthew Morrisroe, F.S.E., Sister Lucia Treanor, F.S.E., Sister Ann Frances Thompson, F.S.E.; and as artist, Sister Mary Roberta Connors, F.S.E.

History of CREative ACTing

"The universe was created in a state of journeying 'toward a perfection yet to be attained.' Creatures were given not only existence, but the dignity of acting on their own, of being causes and principles for each other."[1]

Pope John Paul II

Actually, without being identified as such, CREative ACTing was in a "state of journeying" during my family life as a child. The road map that would give me the sense of direction for the rest of my life was being drafted. I learned at a very young age a sense of direction. There was "my way" and "somebody else's way" that compelled me to make choices—to "take a stand." There was a "right" way and a "wrong" way, a "natural" way or an "artificial" way.

I spent most of my childhood during the historical time known as The Depression. Our family lived on a farm and often experienced natural disasters such as drought, dust storms, tornadoes, hail, and grasshopper plagues. First-hand from my parents, I learned undaunted courage, dedication to one another, and the need to make provision for the future. We children found our enjoyment in simple things such as exploring the meadows and woods for seasonal flowers, birds, and bugs. We made our own toys and sculptures, learned to care for baby animals and to do the chores. These were the years when my creativity was released and problem solving became a way of life. I came to know and value the practical things of life. Unconsciously, I was beginning to "paint my wagon."

During thirty-one years of teaching prior to doctoral research, I met with a wide range of students' learning patterns. These differences made it difficult for many of them to be incorporated within the "fixed dimensions" of our school systems. On the other hand, I found that the vast majority of students appeared to have a strong, positive, and eager response to artistic experiences, especially the dramatic. The reconciliation of these two factors became the subject for my doctoral study at New York University. Here the road map for the first "right of way" named CREATIVE ACTING was designed.

Prior to road construction it was necessary to survey the terrain in order to find an appropriate location. In May of 1972 I was invited to Pocatello, Idaho, to explore the potential of establishing a program of CREative ACTing there. I returned to Idaho in September to further research this possibility. Although the program initiated was privately operated, it gained the affirmation of and related to the Department of Speech and Theatre at Idaho State University, School District #25, Pocatello Community Education Program, the Head Start Program, and the Community Mental Health Program. As director I functioned in a variety of part-time capacities as consultant, teacher trainer, and instructor. While the same types of services were continued the following year, the major emphasis tended toward teacher training. In an expanding phase of the program, in 1973 St. Margaret's School in Blackfoot, Idaho, became a CRE-ACT Laboratory School. Here the faculty was trained in the CREative ACTing methodology and the school became an exemplar. Strong support and endorsement were received from the Idaho State Department of Education and The Idaho Commission on the Arts. Faculty and students demonstrated throughout the state, and as director I served as a consultant and Artist in the Schools not only in Idaho, but in Wisconsin, Connecticut, Minnesota, New York, and Oregon. I also served on various educational research councils on the national as well as the international level.

In May, 1975, CRE-ACT was nominated as Idaho's exemplary educational program to represent the state of Idaho at the National Conference of the Alliance for the Arts in Education at the J.F. Kennedy Center in Washington, D.C. It was one of six schools in the nation selected to bring a representative group of children to share its program.

It soon became evident that the school was ready to establish its own foundation as an integral aspect of the ministry of The Franciscan Sisters of the Eucharist. The first CRE-ACT School opened in the fall of 1976 and was located in the lower level of The First Congregational Church in Pocatello. It began with grades one through three. A new grade was added each successive year until preschool through grade eight were included. As enrollment grew, additional space was needed. In 1981 the school moved to its present location, the former Emerson Public School building, at 526 South Grant Street. This location has served its purpose well since then.

The Pocatello community has been actively involved in assisting the school in its progressive renovation, making it possible to improve the environment for both the students and the community. Exteriorly, contributions have made it possible to lift the asphalt from a portion of the playground, bring in new soil, and get a lawn area with flower beds planted. Community participation likewise has made it possible to progressively "change the face" of the building itself. Heating and electrical improvements, gallons of paint and boxes of tile have transformed various areas of the building. In 2001 the lower level of the school was converted into an Art Gallery in which both students' and professionals' creations are displayed. Another part of this same effort was the renovation of the physical structure of the school library and updating its contents and equipment. The school can proudly boast of a very efficient community "stage crew" who keep the performance area ready for action.

The Franciscan CRE-ACT School is a state-accredited school with fully certified teachers and administrator. The school currently serves children of preschool age through grade six. Experience has proven that transfer to other school systems at this phase of the learning process rather than in the midst of the Junior High level is more feasible. The curriculum encompasses the core subject areas of reading, language arts, mathematics, social studies, and science, as well as visual arts, music, dance, and drama. Classes in religion are broad enough to be meaningful to students of all faiths. A student/teacher ratio of fifteen to one allows students to be grouped into multi-aged classes in which each can progress at his/her own pace, whether that be more or less advanced than that of the other students. Multi-age grouping also affords teachers the opportunity to teach students for a period of years, thus allowing them to tailor their instruction to the long term benefit of the student.

The Franciscan CRE-ACT School serves as the centering not only for the education of its enrolled students, but as a resource, working collaboratively with the community at large in a number of ways:

- All schools and the general public are invited to the Annual Speech Festival and the Annual Dramatic Production.
- The Troubadours, a theatre class offered to high school students once a week in the evening.
- Arts Alive Workshops, daily workshop presentations offered for a week at the school each day featuring one of the following: visual art, music, dance, drama, poetry.
- Evening in Art Performances by professional artists in vocal and instrumental music, dance, theatre and poetry reading; exhibition of wide variety of art works.
- Opportunity for research, situations provided in which teachers may observe, receive training, and where college and university students may conduct their research.

The school has also been favored with visits from a variety of renowned professional artists:

- James Douglas, CBS-TV's Grant Coleman, from "As the World Turns", and his wife, Dawn, an actress and dancer;
- Mercer Mayer, award-winning writer and illustrator of The Little Critter children's books;
- Helen Patton Plusczyk, actress and founder of the "Arts Make Hearts" in Saarbrucken, Germany.
- Amy Ressler Muehleip, University of Dubuque, Iowa, and Founder of Midwest Theatre Company.
- Dr. Theresa Monaco, College of Education, Director, Center for Gifted and Talented, University of Houston, Houston, Texas.

The educative values of this CRE-ACT approach lie in the process and quality of the experience: in original thinking, planning, study, in seeking of information, summarizing material, and putting it into action. One really never "graduates" from CRE-ACT; the performance goes on. This world was created in a state of journeying through sequential phases of perfection. Its process of becoming involves meeting with ever evolving situations, causes, and personalities. We are all collaborators and fellow-workers engaged in the struggle to perfect this world's harmony for our own good and that of others . . . so ACT. . . .

"Paint your wagon" and come along!

NOTE

1. John Paul II, Pope, *Catechism of the Catholic Church* (Liberia Editerice Vaticana: St.Paul Books and Media, 1994), 80 (#302).

Introduction

"Where am I goin', I don't know.
Where am I headin', I ain't certain.
All I know is I am on my way."[1]

Alan J. Lerner, Paint Your Wagon

The format for this book follows the structure of a dramatic production. It begins with a curtain raiser presenting a problem situation, a proposed plan of action for rehearsal, and a description of the performance itself. The theme of the production is developed around three phases of problem solving; namely:

Stating the problem,

Determining a plan of action,

Describing the manner in which the plan of action is pursued.

The author relates this theme to an image used by Lerner and Lowe in PAINT YOUR WAGON. The uniqueness of this process of developing one's personhood is expressed as "painting one's wagon." Then. . . . "Where'm I goin', I don't know."[2] At first sight, this response to one of life's most basic questions reflects a state of confusion, apprehension, and bewilderment, "I don't know." It is a response, however, for which each person takes responsibility.

"Where'm I headin', I ain't certain."[3] Doubt and mistrust are evident, but they are accompanied by a sense of confrontation—"I'm not certain." Yet there is an expression of a need for direction—and then, a description of the manner in which the plan of action is pursued. "All I know is I am on my way!"[4] All I have to know is that I am totally given to the challenge of fulfilling my potential—I AM on my way!

In this publication, the arts-based approach to education called Creative Acting will be introduced to fulfill this need as follows:

Chapter 1 presents the current situation of a restless people engaged in a power struggle to claim their identity.

Chapter 2 takes us back to the pristine order of the universe when the role and charge of the human person was defined. As time ensued, the challenges of change became problematic. The efforts of some leaders who found constructive ways of dealing with change in keeping with man's nature and personhood are presented.

Chapter 3 proposes the CREative ACTing philosophy and methodology as a medium for simultaneously supporting growth of both a people and a nation.

Chapter 4 invites the reader to become actively engaged in the cause and become part of the production. The setting suggests the time and place of each person interested in becoming part of the effort.

Chapter 5 includes in the cast all persons willing to make the journey and to participate in the creative, artistic and dramatic formation.

Chapter 6 concerns responsibilities of the instructor to insure appropriate conditions for performance.

Chapter 7 distinguishes appropriate conditions proper to each level of participation.

Chapter 8 describes an institution in which the proposed approach has been successfully implemented for 36 years.

Chapter 9 takes us on a tour of this institution.

Chapter 10 provides a formal and an informal evaluation of the program.

Chapter 11 challenges the reader to become actively engaged in effecting change by applying the principles and methodology of CREative ACTing.

There is no one road, one way, which will be exactly the same for everyone. That's why we need a road map. Where would we ever be able to "go," what would we ever be able to accomplish, if we were all identical? The key lies in recognizing and respecting one another's uniqueness and potential, and then determining in what ways this powerhouse of energy can most effectively work. We start by recognizing our own abilities, and the strategies we use to best develop them. Then we begin to observe what in others we do not possess or do well, but would complement and enhance our talents. We both invite and explore a collaborative partnership. As it grows we will recognize our need to include more and more people, each functioning in his/her own domain, but united in a single strategy. It can "work," but we must initiate the process. Are we ready?

NOTES

1. Alan J. Lerner, *Paint Your Wagon* (New York: Coward-McCann, 1952), 9.
2. Lerner, Alan, 9.
3. Lerner, Alan, 9.
4. Lerner, Alan, 9.

Section One

CURTAIN RAISER

Chapter One

Struggle for Control in a Confused World

"In the midst of the turmoil of too-rapid change, an extraordinary light has arisen. Factors unique in human history are poised to help us become more than we thought we could ever be."[1]

Jean Houston, *A Passion for the Possible*

Not so long ago it appeared that our world was growing at a pace beyond our control into a single global village. Our ancestors received at birth a pattern for their lives that followed the same ideals as their parents had possessed. They knew the comfort and security of the family heritage and they were satisfied. But then the scene changed rapidly. As many world related events happened between 1945 to the present as in the 2000 years before.

Today's world is very different. It is distinctly divided in culture, faith, wealth and levels of advancement; even more so by attitudes toward power, authority, and cooperation. People who once functioned on a familial trust level are now expected to be part of entities whose concepts and terminologies are unfamiliar to them. Super powers, regional powers, and aspiring powers yield to the belief that only force can bring about a just settlement of affairs. Many persons' best efforts to produce from their creativity and genius have the potential of becoming the means of their own self-destruction. As a result, there is confusion, frustration, mistrust and fear.

NOTE

1. Houston, Jean, *A Passion for the Possible* (San Francisco: Harper Collins, 1998), 6.

Chapter Two

Need for Security and Freedom

"We, the People of the United States, in order to form a more perfect Union, establish Justice, insure domestic Tranquility, provide for the common defense, promote the general Welfare, and secure the Blessings of Liberty to ourselves and our posterity. . . ."[1]

Preamble to the Constitution of the United States of America

A fundamental question needs to be faced: does this kind of progress with man as its author and promoter make human life more human? Is it helping people to become better, more responsible, and more open to others? Are people really happy? For those who are in positions of power, the tendency is not to see things as they are, but as they imagine or would like them to be. For none of us is this a matter of choice. It must be clearly understood that every political and social unit is composed of persons, each of whom possesses fundamental rights that must be upheld and safeguarded. These include the following:

1. The right to life. This right must be marked by a thorough protection of human life precisely when it is at its weakest; that is, at its very beginning and at its natural end.
2. The right to freedom of expression, including freedom to hold opinions without interference, to exchange ideas and information, and to enjoy a free press. The dominion of man over the visible world that the Creator gave him as his task trusts him to respect primacy of persons over things, and superiority of spirit over matter. Man is called to see his own intrinsic goodness and lovableness in all other human beings as well.

What is in question is the advancement of persons, not just the multiplication of things. It is not so much "having more" as "being more." Man cannot relinquish himself nor his place in the visible world that belongs to him. He cannot become the slave of things, of economic systems of production, or slave of his own products. Ultimately, the goal of public policy, its application and interpretation must be not what we "can do," but what we "ought to do"; not what we have the "ability to achieve," but what in our hearts, in our conscience and in our souls we know we "must do."

Given this lack of unity and purpose in today's world, what's next? Where do we go now? We must realize that life is not a destination—it is a journey, an ongoing process of adjusting to the unexpected, of improving, conforming to the right and good. Do we need to retrace our steps and see where we took the wrong turn in the road?

INITIAL ESTABLISHED ORDER

Paul Brandwein reminds us, "There is another view of man. A view of man as human and humane. A view of man in the act of becoming man. Man does not only lose identity; he recovers it. In the geological and historical views of man, the recoveries constituted his immense, never ending journey."[2]

It seems imperative to return to the basic unit of civilization with which we began, the individual person. Not just person "generally," but each with the unique potential that is his or hers, and to rebuild the understanding of and manner of honestly relating to one another. Pope Benedict XVI, with his comprehensive vision of our world, confirmed this approach during a recent interview with broadcasters when he said, "I believe that the real problem of our historical moment lies in the imbalance between the incredibly fast growth of our technical power and that of our moral capacity. . . . That is why the formation of the human person is the true recipe, the key to it all."[3]

Where are we heading? Do we sense the urgency of this challenge? Christopher Frey in his poem, "A Sleep of the Prisoners," encourages us to "take on the cause:"

"Thank God our time is now when wrong
Comes up to face us everywhere,
Never to leave us till we take
The longest stride of soul men ever took."[4]

Christopher Frey, A *Sleep of the Prisoners*

If we are really concerned about effecting a change in our confused world, what is expected of us? Where do we begin?

It is important to recall that at the beginning of time, each element of creation was given its own properties and manner of relating to others, according to its own nature. Man was given dominion over the rest of the world, the task of sustaining the established order. As long as this order was respected, there was peace. In taking on the challenge to restore the proper order to our confused world, Pope Benedict XV1 has given us a natural starting point: the formation of the human person. How does one go about this process?

COLLABORATIVE RELATIONSHIPS

Dependent on the degree to which the potential of relating to others is realized, one human being distinguishes himself/herself from the others. This cannot happen by oneself alone.

> "I am called to be named I am who am, but I am not . . .
> Then someone dedicated with me for life . . .
> Must challenge me to the way in which I am not."[5]

Franciscan Sisters of the Eucharist, *Rhythm of* Transitus

It is crucial not to think of person "generally," but to think of each with the unique potential which is his or hers. A specific heritage, intellectual giftedness, natural aptitude, or experience may be exactly what is needed in order to rebuild the understanding and manner of honestly relating to and working with one another. Johann describes this relationship of man to man as follows:

> To be a man is to be a person. But to be a person is to exist only as an appeal and a response to other persons. Without the other, another who takes an account of me, and for whom my free response means something, I do not exist. . . . But if I need you in order to be myself, you likewise need me. Each of us holds his personhood from the other . . . As persons, we are each of us responsible to and for the other.[6]

R. Johann, "Philosophy"

We need one another's individual aptitudes and strengths complementing each other to increase the potential for reconstructing our world. As Albert Einstein reminds us, "Without changing our patterns of thought, we will not be able to solve the problems we created with our current patterns of thought."[7]

In the new world that lies just ahead, all of these individual skills and fresh solutions will be needed to face the perils and harvest the promise of a technology-driven intercultural world, a new environment, a new world. New birth requires new being, bigger than self. Throughout history, people have felt a yearning to be more. This requires a vision that looks beyond oneself and recognizes the need for others. Where can we find such unprejudiced, creative, energetic resources in numbers large enough to make an impact? Mohandas Gandhi tells us, "If we are to teach real peace in this world, we shall have to begin with the children."[8]

This is our "now moment." I believe that the "way to go" is to our children, our youth, who innately yearn for the challenge and are not afraid to risk. How are we preparing them? It is not enough to imagine the future—we must create it. Jean Houston, in her treatise, *A Passion for the Possible*, gives us the impetus to move in that direction: "Never before have we had so much responsibility for the remaking of ourselves and our world. We seek people with faith in the future of our planet who are willing to develop richer, deeper scenarios of life that involve a new image of a human being and a new style of being human."[9]

When and where can this process of self development begin? Wittingly or unwittingly, it goes on wherever there is human life. It begins "in utero" and continues as long as one lives. If it is not complemented and /or supported by another person, it will develop independently and instinctually, but not with the potential for looking beyond itself. Herein lies the major role of parents and those to whom they entrust the care of their children. These young people need encouragement and support in order to be enticed and involved as they enter into unfamiliar territory.

Caution should be used in the choice of child care and pre-school facilities, primary and educational programs, or special opportunities thereafter. The personhood of each child or youth is at stake. Each is equipped with a specific heritage, characterized by its unique specific strengths and aptitudes. We spend a lifetime developing who we are and a style of living, an outward reflection of inward resources. It is a matter of how we arrange our lives—our human "becomings." Each of us is enrolled full time in the "school of life."

The danger is that we may become discouraged with lack of success when challenged by contrasting situations, withdraw from others, and become "cut off" from the collaboration which is the essential key to growth in personhood. Collaboration is a process of shared creation: two or more individuals with different skills interact to create a shared insight, concept, or project that none had previously possessed or could have come to on their own. This implies venturing into the "unknown" on the part of both, and can imply a threat, but it is an essential aspect of growth.

CHALLENGES OF CHANGE

It is natural to fear being challenged, but there can be a very positive side to experiencing confrontation. If that which is proposed is questioned, ridiculed or ignored, it frequently means others are unfamiliar with or ignorant of what is being expressed. Often, the more ingenuous a proposal may be, the greater the opposition will be. Even when a great contribution ensues, a person may be called a misfit, troublemaker, or rebel, but one can't make a comeback if one "hasn't been anywhere." History has proven that sometimes these are the very persons who have made some of the greatest contributions to society: these are the persons who can imagine, create, invent, explore, push the human race forward, and exert the power to change the *status quo*, and they do.

If students are to succeed in tomorrow's world, their education must instill in them the desire to keep learning throughout their lives. The best way to approach the future is not by attempting to build it in advance. These students are America's future. Only by equipping them with a sound value system in order to prepare them to face and respond to situations as they arise is appropriate.

> "Wonder, wonder, wonder with me,
> Wonderment is fancy free,
> And what we wonder is apt to be
> Tomorrow's actuality."[10]

> Anonymous

For several decades experts have been warning us that to prosper in the future, the United States needs to make much better use of its human resources. This means not allowing people to stop growing at ages 10 or 20 or 30. It means pushing skill-growth up rather than allowing children and adults to coast and stagnate. Over the last decade, reports have provided depressing statistics and conclusions about the status of elementary and secondary education in the United States. During this same period, there have been some improvements, but they have come sporadically and slowly. The No Child Left Behind mandate has a very positive and inclusive tone to it, but it has caused tremendous frustration and anxiety as well. In an attempt to be of service to all, the integrity of the individual person has been lost. Individuals have become "numbers" filling in slots. Utilizing the same norm for millions of students, each of them with diverse backgrounds, aptitudes, and motivation, is an impossible task. Efforts made to perfect it have become less and less effective. Rarely do we hear that students are graduating with more self confidence and love of their fellowmen.

Unfortunately, the major standards of achievement are machine administered and scored, and thus limited in their capacity to measure personal responses. Teachers are threatened with losing their positions if their students fail to "measure up," a fear resulting in "teaching to the test," rather than teaching the students as persons. Uniform time schedules, prescribed methodologies, and use of specified texts and materials prevent the instructors from following their own insights and/or efforts to give a student individual opportunities.

How do we bring a new direction to our educational systems without losing our metavalues? We need master minds bold enough and brave enough to design for our practical world, alternatives which will intrigue not only 5, 10, and 20 year olds, but all persons, regardless of race, color, or creed. Each person lives not only in the "world" created by us for the average student. The other part of each life will be spent in the larger richer world we need to make possible and probable for all.

More than two hundred years ago our country was in a political crisis. Independence was declared; a nation was born. This nation grew and prospered because it was founded upon basic principles inherent in the people for whom it was instituted. Today, our educational system is in crisis and cries for an equally revolutionary change. One of the major factors precipitating the present crisis is resistance to change. Robert E. Weber, New Jersey Department of Education, expresses the problem thus: "The educational establishment is unwavering in its pursuit of the status quo and, if anything, prepares children and youth for a world which no longer exists at matriculation. It does not cultivate future-looking students or even give students the tools they need for invading the future."[11]

Education, as well as government, must evolve from basic principles inherent in the person of the learner if it is to fulfill its purpose. The continued development of man's thinking, his creative thinking, challenges us to consider what he may be able to accomplish, and what his world may become. Our nuclear age is taking us places where old and comfortable ideas no longer apply. Progress such as this requires changes in education: changes that demand boldness, imagination, challenge, and conviction. Today we proclaim that our schools exist for learning. Schools of the future must be designed for learning in a broader sense.

EARLY EFFORTS TO MEET THE NEED

Profound efforts were made by a wide group of educators during the last quarter of the past century to implement this change. Their emphasis was on instruction which would foster creativity and personal instruction. Geraldine Siks maintained that:

The shaping of the future will demand minds which think creatively and which have the vision and imagination not only to seek the answers, but to ask the

questions which science cannot ask. Emphasis must be not so much on memorizing factual materials as on seeking information and using this knowledge in a
creative and constructive way. We must determine how instruction can be used
to focus on the unsolved as well as the solved areas of study. More and more
insistently, today's schools are being asked to produce men and women who can
think, who can find more adequate solutions to impelling world problems, who
can think critically, creatively, constructively.[12]

Another pioneer, Arnold Toynbee, confirmed this viewpoint. "To give a
fair potential to creativity," he says, "is a matter of life and death for any
society."[13]

Creativity is being paid tremendous lip-service by educators and research-
ers, but changes in classrooms which foster creative functioning are extremely slow in keeping pace. Creative activities which often require some
divergent thinking are not only not fostered, but children are often penalized
for attempting to use them. Most of our textbooks are designed to cultivate
learning primarily by authority. Both textbooks and teachers also tend to
focus on what is known far more than upon what is not known. Experimentation or "trying out" is generally fostered only when the teacher can predict
the results.

Richard Courtney emphasized the importance of drama, especially creative
drama, as a means of implementing the change:

Dramatic education is a way of looking at education as a whole. It sees that
the dramatic imagination is the most vital part of human development, and so
it fosters this and helps it grow. It asks that we re-examine our whole educational system—the curricula, the syllabuses, the methods and the philosophies
by which these develop. In all aspects, we must start from acting: not acting
which implies an audience, but acting as improvisation—the spontaneous make
believe inherent in all children. For nothing is alive to us, nothing has reality
in its utmost sense, unless it is quickened and vitalized when we *live* it—when
we *act* it. Then it becomes part of our inner selves. Dramatic education is at
the basis of all education that is child-centered. It is the way in which the life
process develops and, without it, man is merely one of the upper primates.
Further, it provides a necessary "new look" to the educational process of the
20th century. Many of our methods and treatments are derived from systems
conceived a century or more ago. Throughout Western civilization, our young
people are facing problems (social, intellectual, emotional) the answers to which
our present educational system does not have . . . Dramatic education provides
a solution whereby real meaning is given to the child—he has an "end" to his
lessons which is of importance for him because he lives it.[14]

When we review the tremendous strides that technology has made in actu-
alizing the potentials of our material resources, it is difficult for us to believe

that the development of the most important resource of all—the human one— has not kept pace.

NOTES

1. Preamble to the Constitution of the United States of America, www.enchant-edlearning.com/history/us/documents/costitution/-37k- (12 Nov. 2007).

2. Brandwein, Paul F., *The Permanent Agenda of man: The Humanities*, (New York: Harcourt Brace Jovavovich, 1971), 1.

3. Benedict XVI, Pope, "Interview with Four Broadcasters", *Origins*, CNS Documentary Service, Vol. 36, #14 (Sept.14, 2006): 213-220.

4. Frey, Christopher, "A Sleep of the Prisoners". *Dromenon*, 3, 1979.

5. Franciscan Sisters of The Eucharist, "Rhythm of Transitus", Book of Prayers (unpublished)

6. Johann, R., "Philosophy", *America* (September 29, 1962): 816.

7. Einstein, A., "Quotable Quotes", *Positive Promotions* (October, 1999).

8. Gandhi, Mohandas, "Quotable Quotes", *Positive Promotions, Teacher Appreciation Week* (May 7-13, 2000).

9. Houstan, Jean, A *Passion for the Possible* (San Francisco: Harper, 1998), 6.

10. Anonymous.

11. Weber, Robert E., "Human Potential and the Year 2000", *Journal of Creative Behavior*, 2nd Quarter (1973): 135.

12. Siks, Geraldine, *Drama With and for Children* (New York: Harper and Rowe, 1964), 17.

13. Toynbee, Arnold, *Challenge and Habit* (New York: Oxford University Press, 1966), 72.

14. Courtney, *Play, Drama, and Thought* (London: Cassell & Co. LTD, 1968), 44-58.

Chapter Three

Proposed Plan of Resolution

"The traditional goals of education based upon the mastery of an accumulation of wisdom and ideas of the past are no longer adequate to meet the needs of students to be adaptable and capable of managing, developing and resolving situations."[1]

Franciscan CRE-ACT School Brochure

It was through practical experience, first at the elementary, then at the junior high and secondary levels, that the author was swept into this movement. Her concern for unrealized individual uniqueness, and the potential of the arts to relate to its development, became very evident. Simply put, the arts became the "common denominator" into which all categories could be contained.

It was natural then for the thrust of the author's doctoral research at New York University to envision an educational approach which employed not only visual arts, music, theatre, and dance to teach the basic curriculum, but also the use of creative dramatics as the integrating factor and heart of the total educational effort.

This dream fulfilled, The Franciscan CRE-ACT School in Pocatello, Idaho, has served as a center not only for the education of elementary students, but as a resource for the community through its annual production of a scripted play; Annual Elementary Speech Festival; Troubadoures for secondary school students; Arts Alive Workshops; Evenings in Art; and visits with artists, authors, and actors.

CREative ACTing is a recognized form of instruction which involves the total person—physical body, mind, senses, imagination, emotions, power of speech and concentration in the learning process. The techniques employed evolve from basic educational, creative, and theatrical principles applicable to numerous subject areas and learning situations for students of all ages. For teachers, CREative ACTing relates and integrates varying aspects of the curriculum; for students, it is enjoyable because it is practical and relates not only to what "was,", but what "is," and "what could be."

To achieve this end, the curriculum is built on the heritage of the past, accepts the challenges of the present, and projects into the future. It is an approach to building the kind of world which remains not only as a surrounding, but also as a place that a person comes to understand and to which he/she can relate. It includes the arts, which are expressed in terms of the basic elements of knowledge: sound, movement, color, mass, energy, space, line, shape, and language. Math and science, are included, but not to the extent of dominating other areas. Professionals representing a wide range of knowledge and experience are invited to enhance the basic effort to meet the unique potential of individual students. Their participation helps the student to explore the surrounding community in order to experience the world in real life situations.

This is the structure on which the program, CREative ACTing, is built, and the framework from which this book evolves. In order to be of service, a structure must have a purpose which determines its design. The purpose of the CREative ACTing program is to provide the situations which will enable the student to experience life as it evolves in the real world in ways commensurate to that student's ability to comprehend. Its design fosters the concept that life is not static. It keeps growing and changing, looking for new and improved ways of "growing up." It is therefore important to develop:

1. A strong sense of one's identity as part of who one is and from where one comes.
2. Positive attitudes of behavior toward home, school, church, and community.
3. Deep and empathetic understanding of each other.
4. Flexibility and fluency in oral and written communication of ideas.
5. A practiced mastery of basic academic skills.
6. Controlled and balanced emotions.
7. Ability to cooperate, participate and respond in groups.
8. An active creative imagination.
9. Familiarity and competency with, and appreciation for current technologies used in practical learning and living.
10. Initiative, resourcefulness and independence.
11. A sense of stewardship fulfilled in part by developing skills to be used in one's future vocation.
12. An aesthetic sensibility: i.e. a true appreciation of beauty.

Within the total approach are strategies designed for keeping the students prepared to meet challenging situations and to explore creatively new applications for basic facts and principles learned. These skills include:

1. The specific gift of the individual student which is that student's source of energy.
2. The ability to think promptly, creatively, decisively, quantitatively and spatially.
3. The power to write and communicate verbally, physically, personally, and socially.
4. Muscular coordination, physical and emotional control in improvisational situations.
5. Practice in self-discipline and cooperation with others in the creative use of freedom.
6. Knowledge of countless facets of life so that learning becomes experience absorbing actual "slices of life."

The comprehensive scope of this approach provides for the integration of the technical and the aesthetic in our lives. Society is at a stage at which technological developments have revolutionized our way of life. There is a desperate need for the aesthetic to keep pace in order that each person is free to develop human dignity and become capable of living with the world in peace and security.

NOTE

1. Franciscan CRE-ACT School Brochure, (Unpublished)

Section Two

THE PRODUCTION

Chapter Four

The Setting

"All the arts combine in the theatre, décor, the dance, impersonation, effective speech, the song, pantomime, the projection of personality, the art of suppressing self, and even ill will, for the sake of unity of effort. Hundreds of other arts could be listed including the art of living together and the art of creative imagination. That is why the play can never be omitted from child education"[1]

Hughes Mearnes *Creative Power:*
The Education of Youth in the CreativeArts

WHERE AM I GOING?

In order to "set the stage" for the proposal at hand, it may be helpful to clarify some of the concepts that have been presented thus far:

1. There should be no question of place or time—A confused world in the present age!
   Where is it going?
   Where am I going?
2. The action—A summons to restore order!
   Where am I going?
   Am I on my way?
3. The cast—Perhaps not so clear—All living persons, whether one knows them or not, are part of a "whole" greater than oneself. That whole—the entire world—is affected by what I do or don't do, whether I act my part or not. The play will go on, regardless. Like it or not, each of us is responsible for the "whole" and its performance. With this responsibility

a "given," self development will determine the role one has in the performance. Either one acts, or is acted upon. The sooner personal formation begins, the more time and opportunity there will be to make the best use of one's talents.

As one grows older, an expression often heard is, "Why didn't I start sooner?" or "At my age, I should have known better!" The sooner personal formation begins, the more time and opportunity there will be to make the best use of one's talents. Cumulatively, a stronger foundation opens more and greater opportunities for the future; qualitatively, more complex and challenging feats are attainable. The performance never ends—education is a life-long process.

Youth has always been respected and reverenced as a time for wonderful—even magical—things to happen. Older persons have attempted to revive this spirit. In 1503 Ponce de Leon, a Portuguese explorer from the Old World, set out to find the "Fountain of Youth." He crossed the ocean and landed in Florida, USA. What of old Ben Franklin discovering how to "bridle" electricity, Copernicus proving that the world is round? Aaron Copeland continuing to translate the printed symbol into sound in his nineties. These were no longer children, but they kept the spark burning, reverencing and respecting the inner voice urging them on to "more." It is crucial to "kindle the flame" so easily squelched by the automatic, synthetic, and programmed methods employed today.

NOTE

1. Mearns, Hughes, *Creative Power: The Education of Youth in the Creative Arts* (NewYork: Dover Publications, 1958), 92.

Chapter Five

The Cast

"Acting is different from most other arts because actors use their own bodies and voices, rather than tools such as paints or instruments, to create art . . . an actor expresses and creates art through the self."[1]

Katherine Mayfield, *Acting, A to Z*

How prepare an actor for this challenging role? The following principles evolve from the basic concept of personhood and are all inclusive, regardless of age span. The accompanying diagram, THE PERSON, (5.1)[2] images this focus on "person" as the centering force. Emanating from this center are seven aspects of personhood, each of which plays an essential part in the formative process. These will be considered singly at first.

THE PHYSICAL BODY

What image comes to mind when the term *person* is used? One of the first things a child is taught is that each person has a physical body with a number of characteristics in common with every other person.

> On my face I have a nose,
> And way down here I have ten toes.
> I have two eyes that I can blink,
> I have a head to help me think.
> Here's my chin, and very near,
> I have a mouth with which I eat.
> And when I run I use my feet.
> Here are arms to hold up high,
> And here's a hand to wave goodbye.[3]

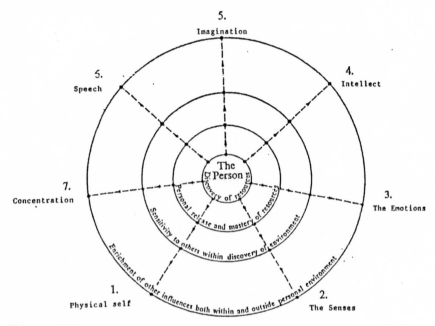

Figure 5.1.   The Person

This is a good starting point, but it is not enough. These are basic com-
monalities, yet it is the differences that identify each as persons and become
the focus in self-identity. The fact that each of us is different becomes
more obvious in working with persons in a group. Not every person has
the same physical strength, the same tone of voice, the same color skin,
etc. There are too many physical variations to validate providing the same
opportunities for all. It is highly significant to remember that any given
body, regardless of physical condition or capacity, plays a critical role in
that it serves as the dwelling place, the abode, in which all other aspects of
personhood reside. Some authors, going beyond the physical proportions
of the body as such, have focused on the suitability and dignity of the body
as a "dwelling place" made sacred by the lived experiences of these aspects
of personhood.

> "Whenever I walk to Suffern along the Erie track
> I go by a poor old farmhouse
> With its shingles
> Broken and black.
> I suppose that I have passed it a hundred times,

But I always stop for a minute
And look at the house, the tragic house,
The house with nobody in it.

This house on the road to Suffern
Needs a dozen panes of glass,
And somebody ought to weed the walk
And take a scythe to the grass.
It needs new paint and shingles
And the vines should be trimmed and tied,
But what it needs most of all,
Is some people living inside."[4]

Joyce Kilmer, *The House With Nobody in It*

The next author shares his view of what he would like a house to be.

"I see from my house by the side of the road,
By the side of the highway of life,
The men who press with the ardor of hope,
The men who are faint with the strife.
But I turn not away from their smiles nor their tears,
Both parts of an infinite plan;
Let me live in my house by the side of the road
And be a friend to men.
Let me live in my house by the side of the road
Where the race of men go by—
They are good, they are bad, they are weak, they are strong,
Wise, foolish—so am I.
Then why should I sit in the scorner's seat
Or hurl the cynic's ban?
Let me live in my house by the side of the road
And be a friend to man."[5]

Sam Walter Foss, *The House by the Side of the Road*

The Senses

Before either the intellect or the imagination can operate, data is needed to work with, to act upon. The senses of sight, hearing, touch, taste smell and movement are the avenues through which basic information enters the mind. The more sensory experiences are provided, the more potential there will be for inter-relating factual data, comparing, contrasting, and constructing new concepts. Because the aspects comprising personhood vary so widely, it is necessary to provide as many kinds of sensory experiences as possible. The senses of sight, hearing and tasting are usually supplied in abundance, but to what extent are the senses of smell and touch used to aid in comprehending? While our technologically developed world brings us into "touch" visually and aurally, and life styles provide countless opportunities to experience tastes, there is a need to experience more concretely and personally the senses of touch and smell.

The Emotions

The emotions introduce the more unique and human aspects of personhood. They are based in feelings and sentiment that are changeable individualized impressions and responses to objective reality and/or other persons. The emotions are called forth more in relation to and as affected by other persons. Because they are based from within, deeply rooted in one's heart and soul, there is a quality of ownership that makes them extremely personal. Recent research indicates that the emotions play a critical role in the learning process. A factor termed "emotional intelligence" has been named to indicate its impact. Although James Abbot is aware that the use of dialogue of this nature is a bold move, he states, "The time has come to look at schools as social laboratories rather than mere knowledge factories. People must be committed to create new ways of working together. Most importantly, people must come to see the need for sharing the intimate knowledge they have about their work."[6]

The Intellect

Just as a mechanism is equipped with controls, a society administered by a charter, or a nation by a chief executive, so the physical body has an intellect that keeps its various functions in proper relationship to one another. This faculty varies widely depending on its experience, natural aptitude, capacity and type of functioning. Intelligence quotients may range high in some categories and lower in others, some persons may be intuitively bent, others experientially; some left brain dominant, others right brain dominant. Because these differences affect the manner in which each person functions both as an individual and in relation to others, it is very critical to consider how they operate. No matter what one does or how it is done—blinking the eyes, solving a math problem, painting a picture, running a mile—it is the brain that controls the action. This remarkable organ provides us with the ability to remember, create, learn, love, hate, feel guilt, sing, dance, and dream.

The left hemisphere of the brain analyzes, abstracts, counts, marks time, plans step-by-step procedures, verbalizes, and makes rational statements based on logic. Because speech and language are so closely linked to thinking, reasoning and the higher mental functions that set human beings apart from other creatures of the world, nineteenth century scientists named the left hemisphere the dominant or major hemisphere; the right brain, the subordinate or minor hemisphere.

The right hemisphere of the brain is intuitive, able to abstract, and imagine. It processes orientation in space, recognizes forms, works acoustically and more holistically than does the left hemisphere. This hemisphere is not under very good verbal control. One can't reason with it. It is not good at sequencing—doing the first thing first, taking the next step, then the next. It may start anywhere or take everything at once. Furthermore, the right hemisphere hasn't a good sense of time and doesn't seem to comprehend what is meant by "wasting time." The right brain is not good at categorizing or naming. It seems to regard the thing as-it-is, at the present moment, seeing things simply for what they are, in all their fascinating complexity. The right hemisphere mode provides a second way of knowing, the ability to "see" things that may be imaginary—existing only in the mind's eye—to dream, to create new combinations or ideas, or recall things that may be real.

These two hemispheres of the brain make compatible neighbors in the human body. However, when they perform the situation is quite the opposite. Our work-a-day world of necessity must adopt and gear itself to the "many." It deals with large numbers of people, products, and provisions—it is forced to systematize. These functions require left brain dominant maneuvers. It is the right brain that modifies, tempers, personalizes, and changes the pace of social routine. Right brain functions are frequently incompatible because they focus on the individual, the variant, the aesthetic, the non-conformist, and the creative. Different as they are, these hemispheres affect the manner in which each person functions both as an individual and in relation to others. It is very crucial to consider them in expecting persons to work together and the manner of task to be accomplished.

The Imagination

The imagination is the gateway to creativity. It is the faculty of the mind that frees one to look at the real world around us from a different perspective, to explore alternate ways of interpreting or relating things, to discover new potentials, to discover the possibilities of change. It is the gift that empowers us to look beyond the drab, the dull, the negative, to the positive, inspiring and magical. It is the gift that helps us realize that we aren't necessarily stuck in a situation—that we can, if we are willing, transpose, alter, reverse, play with the elements, or envision something more appealing.

Speech

Speech is a major form of communication. In making a point or portraying a specific character, the tone of voice and the words we use make a great impression. But speech can be overdone! The general tendency is to do more through the voice than is necessary—to overuse it to "fill the time." This is no longer purposeful communication. Speaking too much and too soon hinders the body from expressing itself.

Concentration

Concentration is one of the most active aspects of personhood. It is the incubation phase, the first step in the creative process, wherein all powers are brought to bear on a project, adventure, or development. Goals are set and strategies for achieving them organized. Concentration may also be a time for assimilating and clarifying the rewards of our efforts. Sad to say, the pace and demands of our culture do not allow much time for this climaxing activity.

ENSEMBLE ACTING

It must be this whole person upon whom concentration is centered. Knowledge and acceptance of self become the stable reference point and basis for security in the process of becoming. The accompanying diagram, THE PERSON, (5.1)[7], shows that all possible points on the circle exist in each person. In the earlier stages of formation, each individual needs assistance to discover and explore his/her own resources. This is a first step. But the process cannot stop there. "The most important single influence in the life of a person is 'another person' "[8] A person's concept of who they are is dependent on the response of other persons with whom they are "in relation." There is a natural and reciprocal need for each to be recognized in relation to the other. Robinson Crusoe needed his Friday;Tarzan his Jane; and Romeo his Juliet. The audience will not believe an actor in his role as a king if the other actors on stage with him do not treat him like a king. When two or more persons are working together, the imagery of one interacts with the other, forcing the other in the very act of creating to new and greater visions. The "ones" make up the "many." In moving outward in the diagram, one can see how the development of the person grows in other dimensions. In the discovery and exploration of one's environment, a growing sensitivity toward other people develops. As one feels the need for enrichment of resources quite outside of oneself and one's own immediate and explored environment, movement continues to the next outer circle. But for each circle, the points remain valid for every individual, and are concerned with existing human resources. This interaction of the individual with the group and with individuals within the group adds dimension to the potential for additional synergetic relationships. Interaction multiplies in effectiveness and makes possible a far greater capacity for fulfillment and production than one could ever reach alone. The function of this procedure will be evident when the use of creative drama is introduced in the methodology procedures.

FORMATION OF THE CREATIVE ACTOR

There is a need to arrange the learner's environment so that processes of involvement will be activated, supported, enhanced, and maintained. The human brain is intensely aggressive and highly unique, seeking out oniy that which is meaningful to it. A brain will admit only that tinput that it decides to admit.

What the brain processes has little to do with what the instructor is doing. Rather, the brain at any particular time is more influenced by its total previous experience in relation to a current situation. Educators should be concerned with the amount of instruction offered to persons who find their dominance in the right side learning area. A broad curriculum that uses both experiential and verbal approaches will more nearly meet the needs of all participants. Both fine arts and practical arts help to fill this need. In claiming to educate the WHOLE person, the CRE-ACT approach takes into consideration the need to integrate learning experiences that bring both sides of the brain into active operation. If one is taught to value all aspects of one's being, to allow more expression of intuitional sensing and feeling and; if one perceives right brain processes as exciting but mysterious, it is possible to explore these processes with a mixture of curiosity and joy. Having options to expand one's awareness, and to make choices about what one wants to say and how to go about saying it, clearly identify oneself as unique, individual, and separate.

There is yet another factor that must be taken into consideration if one is to understand the CRE-ACT approach. No matter how intelligent, capable, studious, or talented a person may be, as long as these areas of knowledge remain distinct from one another, the learning process suffers. Education consists not only in learning what has been discovered, but more so in putting knowledge into different relationships that generate new solutions and resolutions. Creativity, the avenue to the new, improved, the pertinent, must be an integral part of every person's education.

Creative Formation

There have been many attempts to describe creativity as:

1. The ABILITY to produce something that is new, unique, original—something that has never existed before.
2. A PROCESS of bringing something new to birth.
3. Sinking down taps into PAST EXPERIENCES and putting these together into new patterns, new ideas, or new products.
4. The ENCOUNTER of the intensively human being with this world.
5. The ABILITY TO TRANSFER LEARNING concepts and ideas from one situation to another in order to draw a new conclusion, or come up with a new arrangement. The arrangement has a synergistic quality; the combination of ingredients adds up to so much more than the sum of its parts.

These all describe how creativity operates or what it does, but they do not define it. For our purpose, this author prefers going back to a definition which appeared in a supplement to a child's current events magazine over 30 years ago: "Creativity is a PAIN in the imagination."[9]

Creativity is a very specific ability that often relates to "right brain" tendencies. It is essentially a PAIN. The "pain" may be the urge to break out of imposed structure; relieve tension; or actualize inner personal abilities, the price of releasing the personal unique potential within. One cannot be creative without "crossing" an established order; without going contrary to established patterns. Very few enjoy the challenges of change and are much more comfortable in following routine or in the footsteps of another who has "paved the way." Through a creative act, the person becomes one—alone—until that creative expression is accepted by another. Creativity is the ongoing struggle in each person between wanting to write one's name across the sky and knowing only birds and winged creatures fly. It's the struggle between the eye, which can race over hills to the horizon, and the hand that can grasp only what it can reach. It's the struggle between the impulse to express oneself, and the ways in which one has to do it. Creative persons are often puzzled by what is within them. The very nature of their gifts is such that the conventional yardsticks of assessments do not apply. The creative person may be misjudged for being out of line. Creative persons seem to care little for rewards of their insight although eager, even longing, for the approval of those whom they feel may be sympathetic to their particular brand of uniqueness. Often the price is the renouncing, suppressing, or redirecting drives and impulses to bring their behavior into conformity with those whose respect they desire.

Creative persons need to work on their own. They have, to a greater degree than others, the quality of application. Once they have commenced a task, they cannot stop working. And this compulsion, this feeling of "being driven" to complete the task in hand, is very marked. When interrupted they tend to be aggressive, and if it happens too often, there is danger that they may give up entirely.

But a creative person's life is not all negative! Creative people notice things others don't and are more open to their environment. They are more flexible than most, and try a number of approaches, hesitating to fall into rigid patterns of acting. They solve problems in unique ways, always looking for new ways to do almost everything. Creativity thrives on dissatisfaction It MAKES WHAT IS play with WHAT COULD BE. Without creativity, our impossible dreams would never come true. Where would this world be if it didn't have persons unhappy with the *status quo*? The need to create is a healthy part of each and every person. From the time before birth, the child's genetic inheritance and the effect of the environment and personalities upon it, differentiate that child from any other in the whole world. Whether or not this creative ability will remain alive will depend almost completely on the kind of world into which it will be born.

The kind of creativity that parents and teachers promote—that which is the healthiest and most gratifying for the individual—is that which results when positive energies flow as one feels fully validated. It is the creative expression that comes from positive rather than negative sources. If persons are allowed to apply themselves in areas in which their natural abilities lie, their creative instincts flourish and their self-esteem is enhanced as they become affirmed. This energy waits to be freed, developed, nurtured, and channeled into new directions. An act of creation occurs as a result of an individual's endeavors when one strives most fully to be one's true self.

It is the role of the leader, instructor or director to create an environment that encourages and allows positive growth to happen. They need to question, encourage, support and stimulate. It is their responsibility to provide as many resources as possible in order to encourage alternate possibilities. Participants must be taught how to analyze information, how to evaluate cause and effect relationships, how to deal with ambiguity, how to express divergent ideas, and how to explore and take risks.

God has fitted each person to live one life—one's own. There is personal wholeness and joy discovering and using the particular gifts He has given each individual for living that life. Each has one genuine vocation—to find the way to one's self. This is possible only if one stays in relation to his Creator. This makes us collaborators in creation. What each person is becoming is what the world is becoming. The CREative ACTing approach evolves from and incorporates these principles.

> "The weakest among us has a gift,
> however seeming trivial,
> which is peculiar to him,
> and which worthily used,
> will be a gift also
> to his race forever."[10]

John Ruskin, *Modern Painters*

The Artistic Formation

The arts process is an integral part of a creative actor's formation. One of the prime means for attaining this end is to treat all the arts, collectively, as a content area that has the same status and responsibility as other content areas of the program or curriculum. Because both the quality of individual lives and the quality of society are directly related to the quality of our artistic life, there must be concern for the dignity of the individual, and his/her potential for self-fulfillment. Instructors themselves must have a deep and rich sense of the place of the arts in their individual lives in order to be fully alive, vital and in control of the environment and themselves. They need to have the truth—if they are to understand the problems that beset this world, and if they are to understand others as well as themselves.

> Education is learning to grow, learning what to grow toward, learning what is good and bad, learning what is desirable and undesirable, learning what to choose and not to choose. In this realm of intrinsic teaching, of intrinsic education, I think the arts are so close to our psychological and biological core . . . that rather than think of these courses as a sort of whipped or luxury cream, they must become basic experiences in education.[11]

Maslow, Abraham H., *Franciscan CRE-ACT School Brochure*

The arts process has a unique function to fulfill in any context of education. The components of this process are compatible with and conclusive to learning in all subject matter areas at any age level, infancy to old age. They require that the student invest more of the personal self in the process. The simple reason for this is that the components inherent in the arts experience make maximum use of diverse, individualized capacities. They take into account the fact that the person's being affects what, how, when, where and why learning takes place. In this way, they transcend established taxonomies, rigid prescriptions, and traditional theories of learning.

The structure of the arts process assumes a certain human dimension because it focuses on an involved learner. Engagement with the arts is of necessity both personal and active. Evaluation is viewed not only from the point of view of the instructor, but primarily as self-evaluation. A major advantage of the arts process is that it does not depend on contriving ways to involve; it assures involvement because it is naturally involving. It does not have to strive to motivate; it is motivating in itself. The arts help to communicate more effectively because they focus on what is immediate and inescapable. They foster self-expression and provide an outlet for such feelings as sadness, joy, anger and happiness.

Brain research shows that the arts have the potential to expand ways in which the world can be perceived by providing experiences with the natural phenomena of sound, light, motion, time and space—phenomena forming the basis for understanding the world at large. Because they have always dealt with the vital concerns of contemporary man, to bring them into relation with the total curriculum is to assure that the disciplines do not become divorced from the concerns of present day society. Such an approach permits the arts to be viewed as alternative means of understanding subject matter, or processes that at the same time complement and are integral to the total basic educational program.

To understand the concept of the arts in basic formation it is necessary to go a step further; to give attention to what is meant by the word "in" the arts in basic education. The term "in" does not simply mean "as part of." The "arts in basic education" means more than that they become part of the curriculum. It means they are infused throughout the curriculum. Infusion is not correlation. It implies far more than a world cultures course that uses the arts of a people as illustrative material only, or a physical education program that gives cursory attention to dance through square or social dancing, or an elementary program which occasionally allows students to "act out" a story or illustrate student-written haiku for the class poetry book. It means more than an occasional excursion to a museum, theatre, or concert. Art implies a personal, unanalyzable creative power, a skill and proficiency for executing well what one devises or designs as a way of organizing and interrelating knowledge. This subtlety and infusion signifies that the arts should be thought of and incorporated as interdisciplinary studies that are the responsibility of all the faculty. Such a program designed to bring the arts to all participants through all the subject matter states the primary focus of arts education. This philosophy also encompasses specialized arts courses that treat the subject matter of the arts as discrete disciplines. The arts infuse into subject matter, teaching something so wholly new that teachers begin to ask students different kinds of questions and expect different kinds of products. In the final analysis, it is the intensity of the student's learning experience in the arts that will achieve the desired outcomes. A clear-cut conclusion emerges: all the students in our schools ought to be exposed to all of the arts, in a way that enriches the general curriculum.

Dramatic Education

A second environmental factor impacting the educational process is that of dramatics, especially creative dramatics. Dramatic education is a way of looking at education as a whole. It asks that we re-examine our curricula, the syllabi, methods, and philosophies by which these develop, and it encourages starting from acting. Not acting which implies an audience, but acting as improvisation—the spontaneous make-believe in all persons from childhood on. This concept arises from the fact that nothing is alive to us, nothing has reality in its deepest sense unless it is vitalized by living it—when we act it. Then it becomes part of our inner selves. Dramatic education is at the basis of all education that is person -centered. Even the youngest child learns by doing: sitting up the first time, taking the first step, saying the first word. For each of us there is a "first" time for the rest of our lives. As we get older, we are more apt to make sure that the final step or final word is our own.

Dramatic education includes both formal and informal ways of developing personal growth. Formal drama is the expression of thought and feeling in words of the playwright, presented according to his or the director's suggestions for movement and interpretation, and usually intended for an audience. Creative drama is the expression of thoughts and feelings in a person's own terms, through action, the spoken word, or both. Because formal theatre is more familiar to us, it might be better to start there, and then contrast it with informal, creative drama.

Formal theatre, adult and children's, is an art form in which plays written by playwrights are presented by living actors for audiences. The players may be adults and/or children, or a combination of the two. Lines are memorized, action is directed, and scenery and costumes are used. In the formal play, the director, eager to offer a finished project for public entertainment, engages the best actors available and subjects them to the strict discipline required of any creative artist recognizing his obligation to the spectator.

Creative drama, formerly thought of only in terms of children (partly because of the need in formal theatre to memorize an abundance of lines) is currently used at any age level. Professional actors use this technique because of its creative nature and ability to intrigue and mystify. As a rehearsal technique it is also known as improvisation. The elderly use it because it doesn't require much physical activity. Professionals in the normal business world employ its methods consciously or unconsciously to achieve their ends: to call attention to; to emphasize by adding actions to words, to change the pace of transaction, to distract attention from, to embellish, etc. Creative drama is so much a natural part of every human being's manner of expression that it has not been singled out in the past as an aspect of behavior that has a potential to become more useful and effective. Its value as a technique in childhood education received much emphasis in the 1960-1980 period, but with the advancement of technology and the consequent changes in educational methods, its significance has been minimized.

Creative drama provides advantages in terms of personal growth and development that are not implicit in the practice of more conventional forms of drama. It addresses itself to man's basic human behavior in all its dimensions. Learning with all one's being—the physical body, the mind, the senses, the imagination, the emotions, the power of speech and of concentration—summarizes this approach which has as its goal, the personal growth and development of the participant. The techniques employed evolve from basic educational, creative, and theatrical principles applicable to numerous subject matter areas and learning situations for students of all ages. Through improvisation the student learns to make new applications of facts, to "play" with knowledge and find new relationships between facts.

Acting with friends, family, or even with strangers is an every day occurrence. The many masks one assumes during the course of a day may intentionally hide the real self. Pretending to be someone else—to act—is part of the process of living. Because one knows from experience the usual response of a family member or close acquaintance, it is possible to utilize that awareness to one's advantage. It may take the form of joking, asking a favor, threatening, or putting on an emotional response to obtain something. Often these incidents are identified as "putting on a scene." Children utilize tantrums, teenagers manipulate, elderly appease or cajole. Living, understanding and participation are active words that imply immersion in day to day life situations.

The educative values of Creative Dramatics lie in the process and quality of the participant's experience, in original thinking, planning, studying, seeking information, summarizing material, and setting the play in dramatic form. Whether creative dramatics is thought of as an art in its own right or as a tool for teaching other subjects, it means integrating subjects with a "play" at the center and in so doing, helping to make unforgettable certain truths which have significance at the present time. The participant not only imagines, feels, talks about, or thinks about an idea—it is experienced by the whole person.

At the same time that creative dramatics encourages individuality, it develops social relationships. Through a friendly, stimulating environment;

through teamwork and cooperation; and through the sharing of friendly criticism, students learn to develop socially. Creative Dramatics disposes the individual as person to meet unpredictable challenges, to act in complement within inter-disciplinary situations or unpredictable challenges. A very crucial word describing the relationship between society, government, and educators is "partners." This word implies that a complementary relation exists between two, that each contributes toward a common goal; that the efforts of one supports, enhances, and strengthens the efforts of the other. The institution is generally charged with responsibility of imparting the theoretical principle which it is anticipated will find its concrete application in most situations. The role of the two is not identical, and it was never intended to be that way. Neither is self-sufficient, either; each needs the other. Ways must be sought that will make it possible for the two to come together. This approach to education can be one such way of supporting and strengthening one another, our society and our government.

Basic requirements for creative dramatics are few: a group of persons of any age level, a qualified creative dramatics leader or teacher, space adequate for enactment, and an idea from which to create. The principal task of the leader is to set the environment that will evoke a creative response. For this purpose the leader will employ objects, situations, characterization, music, literature, and any form of motivation which will lead the participant from the sensory concrete, through the realms of the imaginative, to the creatively dramatic concrete beyond. Visual stimuli furnish some of the most powerful motivation for dramatization. In giving examples of the manner in which these visual stimuli relate to or inspire creative expression, the value of the initial stimulus will not be accented as much as that of the activity which it initiates, culminating in a new expression—a vision beyond.

NOTES

1. Mayfield, Katherine, *Acting A to Z* , *Backstage Books* (New York: Watson-Gupill Publications, 1998), 9.

2. Way, Brian, *Development Through Drama* (New York: Humanities Press, 1972), 12-15.

3. Primary Poetry, (Unpublished).

4. Kilmer, Joyce, *The House With Nobody In It*, http.//www.poetry-archive.com/k/ the house with nobody in it.html (14 Oct . 2007).

5. Foss, Sam Walter, *"The House by the Side of the Road*, http://www.essentia .com/poems/Roadhouse.htm (6 Oct. 2007).

6. Abbot, James E., "Emotional Intelligence, Part 2," *Association for Supervision and Curriculum Development Newsletter* (Nov.2001).

7. Way, Brian, *Development Through Drama* (New York: Humanities Press, 1972), 12-15).

8. Shafer, Paul D., The MASTER Teacher, Vol. 22, #21.

9. Mitchell, Joan, "Reality", Section 16, Creativity, *Current Events Children's Magazine* (no date).

10. Ruskin, John, *Modern Painters*, http://cc.msnscache.com/cache.aspx?q=72248656283865&mkt=en-US&lang=en-US&w... (14 Oct. 2007).

11. Maslow, Abraham, Franciscan CRE-ACT School brochure, (Unpublished).

What can I say with my hands and my mouth (without audible sounds)?

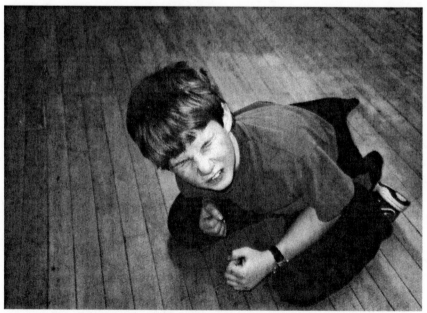

What can I say with my hands and my mouth (without audible sounds)?

What can I say with my hands and my mouth (without audible sounds)?

What can I say with my hands and my mouth (without audible sounds)?

What can I say with my hands and my mouth (without audible sounds)?

One person alone—Classic example of sequential development

One person alone—Classic example of sequential development

One person alone—Classic example of sequential development

One person alone—Classic example of sequential development

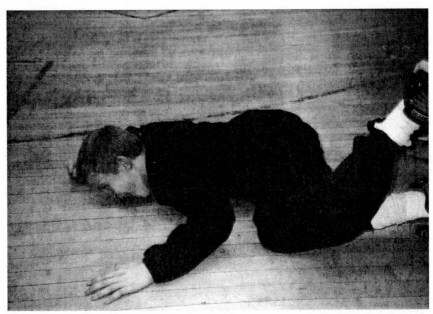

One person alone—Classic example of sequential development

One person alone—Classic example of sequential development

Filling complement space—(two or more persons). "I'll get you!"

Filling complement space—(two or more persons). "Protect me"

How can I fit in? (three or more) "We're in touch"

How can I fit in? (three or more) "We're in touch"

Collaboration—group working together for a single purpose.

Chapter Six

Preparation for Performance

'

All the world's a stage,
And all the men and women merely players:
They have their exits and their entrances;
And one man in his time plays many parts,
His acts being seven ages.[1]

William Shakespeare, *As You Like It*, Scene vii

Given this basic composition of synergic energies present in each and every human being, how do these entities "operate" in the arena of real life? How does each move out, equipped with his/her unique ability/personhood to play a role significant to others and fulfilling to self?

To begin with, it is crucial for each person to come to know who he/she really is, and to be in harmony with the basic design established for the universe, entrusted to mankind from the very beginning, and referred to earlier. This world has had a Director from the beginning of time, and stage managers (kings, rulers, managers, officers) to arrange the set to facilitate performance. The pattern is not new. These roles have been delegated through the ages. Each acting person must "try out" in the rehearsal of real life situations in order to come to know the role that is his/hers. Techniques and situations employed in the process lead to formation of the creative actor. The task of the director (teacher, employer, manager) is to arrange the situations which will provide an opportunity for releasing the natural resources and aptitudes of each person, i.e., to release inner power into productive channels.

This inner power or knowledge begins with facts. Most mathematical and scientific concepts will always remain the same: 2+2 will always be 4; gravity will always keep our feet on the ground; ages of history have been completed. These are "constants." But in creative endeavors one canot be sure where these facts, related to others synergistically, may lead. It is difficult to call creativity into operation at the spur of the moment. No matter how hard one may try, the "spark" one is searching for may not come.

Creativity often requires many trial and error experiences. An appropriate resolution may not be found at a specific time, so a topic may even be "pushed aside" or "swept under the rug" until the matter can be approached with new insights. There are many ways of releasing creative potential and there are many methods courses designed to assist in the teaching of creative skills, but the focus of this text is on one of these specifically—the development of creative dramatics as the heart of a learning experience. Its beat and pulse have the potential of bringing life to all areas of education.

Before beginning with the step- by-step development of principles basic to a CRE-ACT approach, it might be useful to consider some basic conditions/ situations which can make the formation process more productive.

The first step in the process is to "describe" an appropriate settting in which the participants can meet. Roslyn Wilder has identified this as a "space where anything can happen."

> "A space to dream worlds
> that we have yet to build,
> A space to explore the limitless feelings
> we all share,
> A space where I can dare to be
> The people I am
> The people I see
> The people I fear to be
> Or
> The person I might become."[2]

> Roselyn Wilder, *A Space Where Anything Can Happen*

This physical space should have boundaries in order to contain, hold and support the activity. In this space should be only those objects which will/ may become useful during the creative process. Primary teachers often want a corner of the classroom "reserved" for this type of activity. For any age participant, if furniture is moveable, a classroom space can adequately become a forest, a zoo, a senate chamber, one of the planets, a kitchen, a human's brain, or whatever accommodates the need for the curricular content being presented. If a larger space is needed, gymnasiums and auditoriums are usually available. Literally, this space changes with the experience of each participant's life; with the freedom one has to make choices, to imagine, to inquire, to search and to dare in the struggle to attain one's self-identity. The nature of the curricular content and the number of participants usually determine the special need. The topic of distribution of space will be developed later.

The second important condition for preparing the setting for a creative dramatics activity is to develop a suitable atmosphere—one in which people like to be because of its positive climate, support, encouragement, warmth and acceptance. At the same time that an atmosphere is permissive and freeing, it must likewise challenge the participants to approach their task in an energetic and studious manner. A permissive atmosphere is not one in which participants are free to "do as they please." Given the assurance that all individuals are different, there must be provision for varieties of expression and individualistic modes. The atmosphere holds not only a place for equal opportunity, but for varied opportunity. At the same time that diversity is encouraged, there must be a sufficient commonality of modes of expression to form the participants into a community with a purpose. They are members of a class, group, a business, a political party, a government agency, etc. Only by recognizing and incorporating one another's gifts, can something exciting happen.

The most important element in a school with a positive climate is the people. This is one resource which is guaranteed to make a difference. The most important of these is the teacher or leader. This person becomes more of a facilitator or "side coach" setting and resetting the elements in space in order to make possible for participants many learning experiences in which they can create the new and the original. This person need not be a professional actor, musician or artist. Each and every one of us is gifted, as are the students, with the instinct to "play." The teacher's method of instruction turns from one of conveying traditional knowledge in a factual way to a system in which students use their own individual powers in pursuit of various forms of excellence. The teacher prompts and motivates the students to express that to which they most strongly respond. They can and should learn in all possible ways: by voice, by book, by machine, by investigation or by example. Teachers need to keep these differences in mind when creating the environment for specific learning situations. Because the purpose of instruction is facilitated learning, it must be re-emphasized that it is the student who is the learner. It is the student who must do and undo. It is through the learner's activity that one knows learning is taking place.

Before beginning any creative drama activity involving the imagination, it is important to inform the participants of what they are going to do, what will be expected of them, and how the activity will work They need to know beforehand that they are expected to pretend to be other people or work with objects that are not really there. The leader starts with reality and prepares the students for the fantasy portion of the lesson. It is also important to plan an ending which will bring students back to the real world. Sometimes the creative experience may be so happy, so comforting, that a participant may want to continue in it in order to escape the problems of the real world. This prolonged action could lead to a deeper understanding of and possible resolution to a complex situation. When possible, in such a case, it may be worthwhile to return to this topic in order to develop the experience further with other alternatives.

It cannot be stressed too much that the essence of instruction is that the participant learns by doing. A painter learns to paint not only by painting, but by instruction as well. The same is true for a pianist or scientist. Each skill developed becomes not a hobby but a habit—a habit of communication and self-expression. A participant grows in experience as well as in the ability to communicate experience. Tentative concepts are tried on for size. This requires encouragement and support. The participants of these creative experiences are at the core of the process. They are "transformers," converting concepts already discovered into new relationships and new forms of energy so that knowledge is always pulsing, always alive with a positive potential and openness for "more."

Any person of any age who is capable of responding to the direction of the leader and the cohesive effort of the group may participate. This could include 3-year olds as well as 83-year olds. The basic principles governing the approach remain the same, but the manner of implementing them changes with the age and experience of the participants. All, regardless of age, have within them this instinct to "play," which is the basis of participation.

Creating a curriculum is a challenging task. A curriculum must have the power to direct the thoughts and energies of the leader and participants into pertinent and productive channels. First, boundaries need to be set and domains defined. What is the objective to be attained? Will the curriculum be used mainly to teach the basic principles and steps in cultivating dramatic expression, or for personal development and growth? Or will it provide a vehicle for better understanding of curricular content? Only when the objective is clear can creative dramatics bring life, meaning and expression into the effort. Natural, everyday happenings coupled with prepared planning have the potential to build up the tensions necessary to call creative endeavor into action. In order for the creative product to be a useful one, the tension needs to be positive—one that challenges and leads to further developments. Some major examples follow.

METHODOLOGY/PRINCIPLES

Based on the preceding data, theories and insights into the makeup and potential of the human person, five comprehensive principles have been formulated which serve as the foundation for the CRE-ACT approach. Each principle is an essential part of the overall process and should not be overlooked. The nature of the participants, the leader, and the objectives to be achieved will determine the manner best suited for applying these principles. Because each principle builds upon and integrates the one preceding it, there is a distinctive order in which they are to be developed. They are presented in that order here.

1. *Each person determines and/or is assisted to arrive at, a physical and psychological awareness of who he/she is, and to accept both themselves, as well as others, as they are.*

In creative drama, the body itself is the medium of expression. One needs to become aware of the potential inherent in one's body in order to be at ease with using it in acting—to be confident in what one can do, and not to attempt to force that for which one does not have the potential. Experimentation of this nature requires a protective atmosphere. CRE-ACT sessions are not for the purpose of entertaining others or providing audience situations. If there is a valid reason for an observer to be present, that person ought to be invited to become an active part of the session in order not to become a threat to those attempting new experimental forms of expression. Respect for the delicacy of exploring new relationships likewise calls for privacy. Very few are willing to "crawl out on a limb" if they sense that one with whom they are not acquainted is present. Will that person understand? The "trust" element is critical. Experiences and activities for fostering this awareness focus on the theme, "How does my body talk?" and include circle formation and group activities that put the participants in relation to one another. These provide two-fold opportunities: 1) to become acquainted with one another, and 2) to avoid the possible embarrassment of being a sole performer under observation by others. Complimentary and supportive situations develop the awareness of the need for one another.

2. *Every action is (or should be) a response motivated by a directive from a leader, a stimulus, a partner, or a group of persons.*

This procedure keeps the energies of the participant focused and purposeful. The motivation provides a context and a significance to which the student can relate. At first, the relationship is due to the leader's direction. A leader needs to insure and be responsible for providing a medium to which all can respond. After that, the response is usually to a partner. Once one is able to relate meaningfully to another, then there is more potential to find one's place within the group. Anywhere in the process, the response may be to something other than a person: the weather, a stove, a machine, a painting, music, or any other stimulus. The guide to developing this principle is "Why does my body talk?" This movement from a personal centering follows the same general pattern as the diagram of Development of Person, moving outward from a centering as one's experiences widen. Media for promoting complementary relationships include dramatization of opposites, homonyms, compound words, associations, team situations and group formations in which each participant plays a distinct part relating to the whole.

3. *The addition of dialogue to physical action enhances the Power of Communication. Dialogue (speech) adds another dimension to the effort to communicate an idea. Not every spoken word can be classified as "dialogue." Dialogue needs to fit appropriate language with an action or situation. Language gives shape to an experience or a reaction.*

Improvisation is one way to achieve a more natural delivery than the recitation of a memorized script. It is an excellent exercise in learning to "think on one's feet." Little by little the participants develop great pride in their own progress and begin to rely on how much it helps them, not only in dramatic play, but also in everyday contacts.

Listening is important as well. The biggest block to personal communication is the inability to listen intelligently and understandingly to another person. But care must be taken in that this phase of the art is not introduced too soon. The power of speech is one of the basic aspects of personality which one possesses naturally (unless if handicapped in that manner). Participants frequently express a desire to include vocal expression before their bodies are able to respond simultaneously, allowing sounds to "take over" and become a substitute for action. A good norm for evaluating dialogue might be, "How does what I say make what I do clearer?"

Dialogue can be developed step by step. One might begin with sounds (the weather, birds, insects, machinery etc.), then with the repetition of words or phrases found in a story, poem, or descriptive writing; then expression of a given concept in one's own words extemporaneously as the situation inspires one to respond, as in improvisation and problem solving.

4. *Infusion of dramatic principles into the academic curriculum provides a rich resource for activating the dramatic, and a stimulating diversion for bringing factual material to a lived dimension within the academic.*

A vast fund of energy waits to be released in the content areas of the curriculum through the process of experiencing. Once enacted, knowledge becomes functional and not merely theoretical. The student has the opportunity to learn with all one's being—intellect, imagination, senses, body, emotions—and his understanding of the concepts learned is clarified for himself and others.

At this step in the process, instead of thinking of schooling in terms of preparation for the future, the importance of living knowingly in the present— experiencing curricular content—is important and will provide motivation for striving for excellence. Time spent in school is real life, and life needs to be fulfilling and exciting at all times. Participants need to experience the value of their efforts in equipping themselves to live in the present as well as in the future. What one learns now should be functional and operative, no matter what one's age or stage of life is. Each day is a step in the process and serves as a link between the past and the future. The best guarantee for security for the future is to live each moment to its fullest, and to have satisfaction and enjoyment doing it. "Playing" with knowledge, finding new uses and applications for facts, as well as discovering new relationships between areas of knowledge, can be terribly exciting for the participant. Experience and achievement then become a concrete reality, a base from which succeeding efforts find a sense of direction and become an outgrowth, a new development of an integrated whole rather than an isolated entity. The media for implementing this principle are endless. The more trite and uninteresting the curricular content, the greater the challenge to find new and exciting ways of exploring it.

5. *Creative exploration of alternative uses and application of subject matter and facts learned challenges us to continue the work begun by the Creator, unveiling inherent potential in created matter not yet disclosed.*

The real test of a good education is the ability to discover new insights to implement what one has learned. If the curriculum is thought of as fuel, and imagination as the spark, then improvisation and creative problem solving become the fire that gives off light and energy for new growth and development.

Today there is a great need to be able to work creatively with facts; not just to memorize them, but to find new applications, new uses for, and new relationships between. This is the way new discoveries and inventions are made. The future of our own lives and our nation will depend on our ability to be creative. During the coming decades care must be taken to develop not only technological resources, but human as well. Educators must challenge students and encourage them to look at the world around them in new ways. Early in childhood is a prime time to begin the development of these positive qualities. Young children are experts in everything! No matter what they are asked to attempt, they will say, "Sure!" They are full of natural ability and self-confidence.

This stage of learning can be both challenging and enjoyable, but it must be nurtured and cannot stop in the nursery or elementary school. Instead of being restricted to the usual educational tools and materials, opportunities must be given to choose from not only content, but also method, place, space, equipment, resources etc. The prime time in this process might be compared with a "hole in the sky" establishing new boundaries and a freedom not previously experienced.

The resources and instruments for fulfilling this principle are human beings—people whose personalities and potential have been freed to become persons they are intended to become—a creation, continuing in process, as the personality emerges step by step. The formation of a personality that is creative depends on the experiences one has or chooses to have in developing that personality. This brings "full circle" the process of education whose ultimate goal is the development of the unique personhood of each individual in all its aspects of the creative actor.

NOTES

1. Shakespeare, William, "As You Like It", Scene vii, *The Works of Shakespeare* (New York: Hamilton Book Co., 1911), Vol. 1, p. 69.
2. Wilder, Roslyn, *A Space Where Anything Can Happen*, (Charlottesville, VA., New Plays, 1977), frontes piece.

Chapter Seven

Rehearsal

"When will I be there, I don't know,
When will I get there, I ain't certain,
All I know is I am on my way."[1]

Alan J. Lerner, *Paint Your Wagon*

Are you with us yet? Have you decided where to go to "stake your claim?" There are numerous areas waiting to be discovered, uncovered, or recognized. This is not a matter of "ABC's or $\prod r^2$ or getting a Ph.D. Where in this universe is your "gold mine?" Opportunities are endless! The major areas of your search will be mapped according to chronological age and/or physical capacity. One may hope that you will be prompted according to the direction in which your gift, your personhood needs companionship.

Regardless of your area of interest, and applicable to any situation you may choose, there is one basic principle affecting all ages/situations which cannot be ignored, namely, Creative Acting is body-based. The body is the "abode" of life—it holds life within. Most entities are embodied in a specific way: a picture is framed; a plant is concealed in a bulb or seed, an egg in a shell, Every aspect of creation has its own form and manner of functioning. Regardless of whether the entity is alive or an object for man's use, there must be an honest relationship in relating to them. Try putting a gallon of water into a cup, or watering your lawn by the spoonfuls. Try heating and lighting your house in winter with a candle. Try using your car key to unlock your house: do these odd couples work together? Is it always easy to find this relationship? This is why we are offered a variety of foods, clothing styles, a whole range of videos, thousands of different styles of houses and automobiles. How is this principle being applied in human development?

51

There is a natural response of human body to the material body. Some persons learn better by doing; others by observing; some by reading, others by writing, some by discovery on a field trip, others by listening to music. This interaction of the person with the medium best suited /used is the secret of human fulfillment. It can be baffling for the teacher who is expected to use the identical materials for her class as every other class in the same building, district or state. The same problem faces leaders and employees in any public situation.

GUIDELINES FOR APPLICATION OF PRINCIPLES

Because of this wide range of individual differences and/or needs, it is absolutely necessary for each organization, establishment or group using the Creative Acting principles to draw up a curriculum specifically designed to meet its perceived need/purpose. To fulfill this need, it is wise to establish a position of curriculum coordinator.

From the beginning of this text, it has been emphasized that education is a lifelong process for everyone, and that the creative acting principles can be effectively applied at any level. A few pertinent guidelines for curriculum development at the more generally recognized educational levels of formal and informal educational settings follow. The last section of this book will present The Franciscan CRE-CT School, the prime exemplar of the Franciscan Creative Acting Program. Watch the signs, keep your directions straight, and keep on moving, There's gold in them there mines!

FORMAL EDUCATIONAL SETTINGS

Pregnancy

The philosophy of CREative ACTing pertains to the entire life span of a person, beginning with pregnancy. The infant body knows through vibrations the parents' involvements. All routine household and family activities should be approached with this concept in mind. Parents should engage actively and passively in customary and creative ventures so that not only physically, but emotionally and psychologically the child will be exposed to creative and aesthetic influence.

Infancy and Childhood

The new-born child is guided through early stages of body awareness to discover his own uniqueness and identity. As his powers of thinking, feeling, sensing and intuiting are brought into balance, his selfhood is freed to develop. The surroundings of the child should be, in as far as possible, characterized by a positive atmosphere enriched with the honesty of natural materials and aesthetic experiences. Toys, when possible, should be made of natural materials in order that a child will come to know the integrity and wholeness of basic substances. Poetry and prose should be read to the child. Outdoor experience should be frequent. Through witnessing the rhythms of nature working together, the child can discover more easily that which in one's own being is natural and authentic. A child should have an animal to which he/she will learn to respond. Animals do not feign or "cover up" as humans do. Thus a child can observe types of responses that correspond to his behavior, and the manner in which to better relate to other people. They love to imitate Mama and Daddy.

Elementary

Little children want to play. The key to involving them lies in sharing simple dramatic experiences that hold high appeal. They live close to their environment and their interest center around the real world in which they live. They find much more enjoyment in such active and impressive things as trains, cars, boats and a variety of animals than they do in sitting quietly and making sounds. A child's ability to discriminate grows through such experiences as becoming a train engine that moves fast or slow; a train with a light load or a heavy one; a train that has a big or a little engine; a train that whistles with a loud or a soft whistle; a train that is near or far away, a train that is a diesel, electric, or heavy freight.

There should be more involved experiences with soil, plants, animals, and humans through which the child will come to know who he is and his manner of responding to other persons and situations. These experiences should be directed toward piquing the children's curiosity, encouraging them to ask questions, to explore and to discover. These are the bases for igniting creative potential.

Field trips into the community are not completed until they are followed by critical discussion, evaluation, and creative problem-solving projections. It is important to witness theoretical principles in action and in context. One of the greatest incentives for a student is to see that what is being taught is functional.

Junior High School

Major changes frequently take place at this level. It must be kept in mind, however, that as crucial as a school's surroundings and environment may be, no advances in policy, no acquisitions of new equipment, have their desired effect unless they are in harmony with the nature of the student and are fundamentally acceptable to him/her.

The essential domains of human experience and thought embrace much more than the array of subjects conventionally allotted to the curriculum. There is a need to transcend these rubrics in order that students might get a holistic picture of the universe about which they can inquire and be conversant.

Creative dramatics prepares for participation in formal drama and can be profitably used:

1. In tryouts, mood may be set with music. Short scenes may be played with spontaneous dialogue after the script has been read.
2. Formal scenes may be temporarily turned into improvisations in order to achieve naturalness of expression.
3. Improvised dialogue may be developed in crowd scenes.
4. It is a natural opportunity for practice in purposive speech as an instrument of expression, and also in its technical aspects, involving good diction, confidence, audibility and clarity.

Senior High School

Creative dramatics, usually incorporated into other forms of drama and theatre at this level, can serve as an integrating factor in many avenues of learning. Hugh Mearnes expresses this well, reflecting on his own experiences: "All the arts combine in the theatre: decor, the dance, impersonation, effective speech, song, pantomime, projection of personality, the art of suppressing self, and even ill will, for the sake of unity of effort. Hundreds of other arts could be listed including the art of living together and the art of creative imagination."[2]

During these years, students should become involved in computerized and technical methods of communication, e.g., filming, journalism, and becoming conversant in group expression.

College and University

Those pursuing theatre at this level usually direct their efforts to focus on either of two alternatives: either they make it a lifetime career for personal fulfillment through performing for others, or they use it to instruct, direct, or assist others who are interested in developing their talent. In either dimension, drama becomes a medium for exerting a wide influence on society. How does this happen?

1. In enacting a character, people have to work out the lives they are pretending to live in another way. So drama demands cooperation.
2. People have to employ what they already know about the life they are trying to live. So drama puts life experience to use. It makes factual experience (information) come into active development.
3. People have to be able to live in two worlds simultaneously—their real life role and the one they are enacting, So drama uses fiction and fantasy, but makes people aware of reality.
4. People have to agree to sustain a common understanding of what they are making together no matter how differently they may appear to be thinking. So drama stresses effort to sustain mutual support for one another while allowing people a chance to work differently—to bring personal ideas to the whole.
5. People have to express thinking and feeling actions to each other. if they don't, then no one in the drama knows what is going on. So drama makes people find precision in communication.
6. People have to interpret the actions of others, but often in unfamiliar circumstances. (You don't meet dragons every day; you don't have to argue with magicians, face the rigors of journeys, or cope with enemies who seek your life). So drama tests your ability to live out crises. It tests your attitudes and your present capacities.

This should be a time of specialization during which the student moves out of the orbit of his previous centering to learn new facets of his preferred area of research. Because the medium of drama is accentuated in all levels of this effort, it is highly recommended that all students spend some time in Greece where drama was so basic to education and where it played such a dominant part in the daily life of the Greek people.

INFORMAL EDUCATIONAL SETTINGS

School buildings are not the only places where education takes place. Some persons, because of physical, emotional or mental disability, may not even be able to attend an established educational environment.

Learning disability, as the name suggests, may be a problem intimately related to education and classroom practice. Persons with this inability display difficulty in the fundamental processes by which information is obtained, stored and organized. Among the fundamental information-gathering processes that are disturbed is the perceptual-motor process. Persons in this category do not see as we see; they do not hear as we hear; they do not make movement responses with the same continuity with which others do. Both on the input level of perception and on the output level of motor response, their handling of information is disrupted. This disruption is not due to failure of sensory organs to deliver information; nor is it due to failure of muscles to respond. It is due, rather, to a disturbance of the processing of information by the brain and central nervous system. Whether one works with children who are gifted intellectually or with those who are struggling to figure out where they can fit into the mainstream, or with children who are challenged visually, auditorally, cognitively, physically, or emotionally, we know that within each one of these lies a core of personhood that yearns for expression in a way that can be appreciated and welcomed. This feeling of self-worth is a critical part of the learning process. The United Cerebral Palsy Association has so clearly stated, "The arts have many special values to people with disabilities, but one of the most important is a method of expression sometimes not possible by any other means. The arts are intellectual disciplines requiring complex thinking and problem solving that offer opportunities for students to construct their own understanding of the world."[3]

Experiments have shown that body manipulations employed in action plays have helped the physically handicapped. The blind and victims of cerebral palsy have been helped to achieve a greater degree of coordination through body movement. The repetition of sounds, especially those found in literature, tongue twisters and syllable combinations, is an aid for those with speech problems. The action plays are invaluable for mentally retarded children. In the activity of play they often lose their fear of making mistakes and begin to act and speak simultaneously, which is a great achievement for them.

Because music therapy is a non-threatening medium, unique outcomes are possible. This therapy includes the use of behavioral, biomedical, developmental, humanistic and adaptive music instruction. The therapy is used to treat an array of developmental disorders including Down syndrome and attention deficit hyperactivity disorder, as well as to help abused children. Musical aspects of reciprocity in shared play, turn-taking, listening and responding to another person can be augmented in music therapy with children with autism to accommodate and address their frequently avoidant styles of communication. Autistic children have made enormous strides in eliminating their monotonic speech by singing songs composed to match their rhythm, stress, flow and inflection of the sentence followed by a gradual fading of the musical cues. The power of music can transform lives significantly. The classics, new-age and folk music seem to be more effective than other forms. Baroque and classical particularly make the cognitive process more effective.

These may seem like minimal achievements, but they are positive steps in the building of personal potential. A positive endeavor, as expressed in the following lines, is a step in the right direction.

> "I am only one, but still I am one;
> I cannot do everything, but still I can do something;
> And because I cannot do everything
> I will not refuse to do the something
> That I can do."[4]

Edward E. Hale

People in old age are very interested in music, although many of them have weakened hearing or other old age shortcomings. Through music it is possible to reach vividly pleasure-giving memories and meaningful experiences connected with earlier phases of life, which could otherwise remain out of reach. Music seems to push traumatic and distressing meaningful experiences aroused by it to a distance. Copeland explains, "There is something in music that keeps it as if at a distance even at the moment when taking us into its embrace. It is simultaneously absent outside us, and yet it is an inner part of ourselves. Even though it shakes us profoundly, it is at all the time under our control."[5]

NOTES

1. Lerner, Alan J., *Paint Your Wagon* (New York: Coward-McCann, 1952), 9.

2. Mearnes, Hugh, *Creative Power: The Education of Youth in the Creative Arts* (New York: Dover Publications, 1958), 92.

3. United Cerebral Palsy Association, http www.neld.org .www.Autism.org (15 April,2007).

4. Hale, Edward, The MASTER Teacher, Vol. 22, #21.

5. Copeland, A.http://www.voices.no/main issues/Voices 2(1)lchtonen.htm (15 Apr., 2007)

Section Three

THE PERFORMANCE

Chapter Eight

Exemplar:
The Franciscan CRE-ACT School

"Got a dream, boy?
Got a song?
Paint your wagon
And come along."[1]

Alan J. Lerner, *Paint Your Wagon*

The dream was vivid! It became a basic "script" in hand! But where was the stage? The production crew? The road wasn't well marked yet and required considerable "wandering." The "stars" were in the heavens, but so many and so far away. After two years of "wandering" across the United States from coast to coast searching for a place to "stake a claim," an invitation was extended by the Public Relations and Theatre Departments of Idaho State University to come to Pocatello, Idaho to explore possibilities for the future. This required a series of "diggings," searching for a favorable site. During this time, the founder functioned in a variety of part-time capacities as consultant, teacher trainer, and instructor. She conducted Creative Arts workshops in Minnesota, Oregon, Iowa, California, Tennessee, New York and Utah. During the school year 1973-1974 the major emphasis tended toward teacher training and development of a laboratory school in nearby Blackfoot, Idaho. In May, 1975, the CRE-ACT program was nominated as Idaho's exemplary educational program to represent the state at the National Conference of the Alliance for the Arts in Education at the J.F. Kennedy Center in Washington D.C. It was one of six schools in the nation selected to bring a representative group of children to share its program that October. This affirmation indicated clearly that the "gold" was to be found in the hearts and minds of the children themselves. It prompted the opening of The CRE-ACT School, a private school sponsored by The Franciscan Sisters of the Eucharist and open to persons of any race, color or creed. The school was first located in the lower level of The First Congregational Church, 309 N. Garfield, Pocatello, Idaho. At its opening the school served students of grades one through three. A successive grade was added each year. This modest beginning located in a single room of the First Congregational Church is presently housed in the former Emerson Public School, the oldest elementary school structure still in use in the city. The building's age invites frequent "breaking" of the set to allow for creative renovations.

STRUCTURE AND ORGANIZATION OF THE SCHOOL

Where is the Franciscan CRE-ACT School? It can't be missed if one travels west on Pocatello, Idaho's South Overpass, Benton Street, over the Portneuf River, to the corner of Benton and Grant Streets. The traditional two story rectangle red brick building, flanked on three sides by the playground, covers the block. It is conveniently located not far from the city's business center, higher education center, and medical center.

The production staff includes the principal, the classroom teachers, artists, secretary, and teacher assistants as needed. Each is required to make a commitment to learn and to use the CREative ACTing principles and methodology in their position. For those who have not had an opportunity to enroll in the course taught in a formal educational setting, private in-service is arranged. Monthly in-service sessions are arranged for the entire staff to insure proper understanding of new developments. The meetings also provide opportunities for the staff to offer suggestions for introducing new procedures or altering existing ones.

The age span of the student body includes preschool through grade 6. Preschoolers and and kindergarteners occupy self-contained classrooms, while older students in grades one through six, divided into multi-aged groupings, move from a homeroom to various classrooms. These classrooms are designated in terms of curriculum content, with each age level and grade using them according to their ability. Within these multi-aged groupings there are still additional flexible divisions. Students of varying cultures perceive and learn differently. Or a student may have already experienced information that is new to another student. The subways and skyways of New York may be new to Hank, whose home has always been in Idaho's desert, while the metropolis was Brenda's home for eight years. Fred, reading at a fourth grade level, might calculate problems at a seventh grade level. Diversities such as these frequently cause grade lines to disappear. Adjustments to these

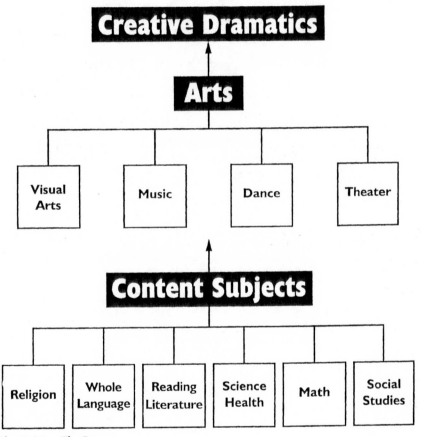

CREATIVE ACTING
THE ENTIRE PROCESS

Creative Dramatics

Arts

| Visual Arts | Music | Dance | Theater |

Content Subjects

| Religion | Whole Language | Reading Literature | Science Health | Math | Social Studies |

Figure 8.1.   The Process

variables free students to progress at a pace natural to them with minimized opportunity for boredom.

As the accompanying diagram (Figure 8.1) shows, the school provides, in the first place, the basic academic subjects required for all elementary schools. In addition, experiences in visual art, dance, music, and creative drama are offered to all. These arts collectively are considered an integral part of the basic educational program with the status and responsibility of integrating and clarifying traditional academic subject matter.

But, at CRE-ACT, there is still more. The art of creative dramatics performs a two-fold function. First, in its own right, it injects a creative element into the manner in which the students process their knowledge. Secondly, as a methodology, it becomes the pulsating beat integrating both the arts and the academic curriculum into a unified process.

> Dramatic education is, therefore, not merely a way of looking at the educational process (a philosophy), or a way of helping the individual to develop (a psychology) or of assisting the individual to adjust to his environment (a sociology); it is the basic way in which the human being learns—and thus is the most effective method for all forms of education.[2]
>
> Richard Courtney, *Play, Drama, and Thought*

Because of combinations of grade levels into multi-aged groups, curricular content is arranged in three cycles, each focusing on a different theme and covering one scholastic year.

Cycle I—Community
Cycle II—Conservation of energy
Cycle III—Stewardship

In this progression, the focus is first on the student as a member of a group to which he belongs. He is not alone and learns to relate to others. At the second level the student is faced with the problem of saving time and energy through grouping. Not everyone needs to do everything! At the third level, students begin to think in terms of leadership and responsibility, according to a person's natural aptitude. In this arrangement, any student is able to complete in six years the academic content projected for those grade levels. However, over and above that, the theme of each of these cycles determines the curricular content to be taught each year. This includes the selection of field trips, the types of professional services to be invited to the school, textbooks and materials to be purchased, and even the choice of the scripted play to be performed at the culmination of the school year. Within this general format, how does CRE-ACT function?

"Curriculum is the fuel,
Imagination the spark,
Improvisation/problem-solving the fire.
Come and warm yourself!"[3]

Franciscan CRE-ACT School Brochure

Parents have a vested interest in the school they have chosen for their children. It is their school as well as their children's. They are expected to participate in the school's activities and promotions. CASPA (CRE-ACT School Parent Association} meetings are held at the natural major divisions of the school year and as often as is helpful to co-plan with the staff. Most parents bring their children to school because bus service is not provided. Some take time to walk their children into the building, helping to carry a "prop" for science class, or to "get a peek" at a project in which their child has participated.

Are the students in "uniforms" or "costumes?" The answer is "both." The similarity implied by uniforms consists in the personhood that each child brings to be developed—the living spirit waiting to be released and formed. The "costume" evolves from the interaction of the person with the school environment. The student's self-identity assumes expression in relation to "others": persons, places and experiences which are part of daily life. "Costume" is reflected not only in style of clothing worn, but also in aspirations, behaviors and character development of the student. The child who says in grade four, "I'm going to Hollywood to become an actor," exhibits a determination that "clothes" and characterizes a further manner of presenting the self in daily routine, particularly in physical appearance, personal appeal, and honesty of impression. A student whose dream is to enter the medical or nursing profession will focus on cleanliness, proper diet, and concern for children injured on the playground. The natural pace of physical, emotional, and social development shows change in areas such as muscular energy, degree of security, and number of friends. Just as a costume motivates one to take on a character, so these factors stimulate a student to grow into and become that which he/she envisions, as expressed in the following lines:

"Let me grow as I be
And understand why I want to grow like me;
Not like my Mom wants me to be,
Not like my Dad hopes I'll be
Or my teacher thinks I should be.
Please try to understand and help me grow
Just like me!"[4]

Fleming, *Bill of Rights*

NOTES

1. Lerner, Alan J., *Paint Your Wagon* (New York: Coward-McCann, 1952), 9.
2. Courtney, Richard, *Play, Drama, and Thought*, (London, Cassell and Co .LTD, 1968), 269.
3. Franciscan CRE-ACT School brochure, Unpublished
4. Fleming, edited by Marcia Lloyd , *Adventures in Creative Movement Activities* (Malaysia:Federal Publications Sdn. Bhd. 1990), 3.

Destination: The ugly duckling
Your name: Jessie

1. The main idea of the story is... if people think you are ugly does not mean your dumb!.
2. The setting of the story is... On a farm and in a pond.
3. The main characters are... The ugly duckling, other ducks his brothers and sisters and his mom.
4. The problems the characters have to overcome are... that the duckling isen't ugly.
5. The good in the story is... that the duckling didnt stay ugly.
6. The bad in the story is... that he was made fun of.
7. A famous quote from the story is... you are the uglyest duckling I ever saw
8. The magic used in the story is... none
9. My opinion of the story is... I liked the story and the duck.

The Ugly Duckling

SHOW YOUR FEELINGS

SAD
Ugly duckling
because he was
ugly.

WORRIED
The mother duck
becaus at the beggoning
the ugly ducklings egg didlent
hatch.

HAPPY
his brothers and sisters
becaus they worn't ugly.

ANGRY
the other ducks
because he was
differant.

The Ugly Duckling

Wanted

porridge thief
age.6
50,00,0$ 59¢ Grand prize
Call 239-9807 for detels

Goldilocks

If you see this man
Call 911

Needs a bigger heart

WANTED

Scrooge

Chapter Nine

Performance Areas

"We are the hero of our own story"[1]

Mary McCarthy

The facility is a traditionally designed early nineteen hundreds two-story school building with four classrooms, two on either side of a central hallway on each floor. For CRE-ACT, these rooms are areas of space which in the course of teaching are designed and redesigned as spaces where "anything can happen." The aspect of curriculum to which each space is given designs that space. A legend to the blueprint might list them as:

CURRICULUM AREA	SPACE AREA
Language Arts	Script
Religion	Dressing/Makeup
Social Studies	Costume
Mathematics	Prop Room
Science	Back Stage
Physical Education	Warm Up
Visual Arts	Design
Music	Sound
Dance	Movement
Drama	Rehearsal
Pre-School/Kindergarten	Try Out/Audition
Principal's Office	Stage Manager
Director	Green Room

Each instructor might be likened to a stage manager in his/her own right, who "sets" and "resets" the space as students become acquainted with the tools, their uses, and their potential. Not only are students prepared for the future. Their education is for NOW and becomes an integral part of their present life. In drama the term for this experience is "slice of life." Experiencing this moment, this "now," awakens in the students the drive to explore and improve their society, to envision worlds yet to be built. They need to know a freedom to go beyond established boundaries and present limitations. This is the task of CRE-ACT. Challenging? Yes! Possible? Again, yes! The Creative Dramatics method of instruction is a key capable of unlocking such resources.

A significant part of each classroom is the large carpeted area which becomes the arena or stage on which most of the group activities are presented and "bounced off" on one another. Moveable chairs and desks provide flexible space areas for study, research, composition and group work. Textbooks and the classroom library furnish an abundance of materials for scripts. Educational supplies become props, and the computers become a technician's haven. Optional features such as works of art, plants, guinea pigs, puppets, and masks often become part of the performance. Handmade "playbills" sometimes announce coming features.

How does a typical day at CRE-ACT begin?

THE ASSEMBLY

"A word fitly spoken. A word miraculously written. Such words have power to move mountains, to change history, to sway the human heart, and how does it come about?"[2]

Editors of Read Magazine, *Words, Words, Words.*

After checking into their homerooms, the entire student body assembles in the hallway and sits in a semicircular group on the floor. Because CRE-ACT incorporates students from a variety of ethnic and religious persuasions, it is important to make sure that the uniqueness of each person is respected and is free to develop within the CRE-ACT atmosphere. The purpose of the assembly is to assist the students to integrate what is currently happening or anticipated to happen into their character and personal growth patterns. The assembly is usually conducted by the principal or a faculty member, but it is an excellent opportunity for a student to introduce an initiative which has been approved by the administration. The theme for discussion may focus on anything from the headlines of the newspaper to a seasonal or liturgical event, the procedure in the lunch room, a disagreement on the playground, or a letter of congratulation to the winner of an art contest. During the time of the all-school play rehearsal, lines from the script are often used to get a better understanding of their meaning and to challenge living into their message. For example, the year in which *SNOW WHITE* was the play chosen for student production, on a given day the focusing question was, "Are you the Queen?" A period of silence ensued. Children looked at one another. Did they want to be identified with a character portrayed as wicked? Just what did the character of the Queen in *SNOW WHITE* mean? The students came to the conclusion that they were kings or queens, and that each had a domain of his/her own. The task of identifying those domains became the thought pervading the day. During ensuing sessions, the nature of these domains and who and what inhabited them were probed. Perspectives reached during such a morning assembly help students as a body to focus on specific topics for consideration of attitude or behavior each day and to motivate them to make these qualities operative in their lives.

Students are encouraged to suggest possible topics for consideration during assemblies. Some come to the level of trust that allows them to share situations in which they feel mistreated or short-changed, such as name calling or being teased unduly. With the challenge set for the day, students move into classroom spaces. For first graders, who the year before were in a self-contained classroom, joining the main "circuit" of moving from room to room is quite a challenge. Learning to stay "on line," carrying their equipment with them from room to room has its problems to begin with, but the children do get their "act" together with a sense of pride before long.

As we visit the curricular oriented areas, some examples will be given of the manner in which the CRE-ACT principles may or have been applied to the various aspects of the curriculum at the Franciscan CRE-ACT School. It is crucial, however, to remember that in order to be effective, the type of experience offered or made available must always begin with the participants and be utilized according to their ability, specific need and appropriate timing. It can never be presumed that a specific aspect of a lesson will be presented on a specific day. What is presented in this text are practical examples of the CRE-ACT theory in practice, but appropriate timing for their use is critical.

CURRICULAR ORIENTED AREAS

The Tryout Room

The Pre-School and Kindergarten Space

> "The main part of intellectual education is not theacquisition of facts, but learning how to make the facts live."[3]
>
> Oliver Wendel Holmes, Jr.

In keeping with the design and spirit of theatrical production, the Preschool/ Kindergarten space is named The Tryout Room. Tryouts or auditions are held before casting a performance to test persons desiring to become part of the production. There are some general characteristics of children at this age level which give some assurance that they will fit into and profit from a performance-oriented approach to education. "Performance" at this stage does not necessarily refer to acting before or entertaining an audience. The term as used here refers to utilizing theoretical or abstract knowledge in a concrete manner.

From the viewpoint of the individual person, children ages four through six learn by doing and applying what they know. They learn basic concepts such as how to follow directions, take turns, share materials, listen, and how to center these activities in their physical bodies. Socially, they learn how to converse with others, how to listen, how to make and keep friends, and how their actions affect other people.

Performance skills, such as drawing, writing, counting and dramatization, are learned through games, songs, use of manipulatives, dramatic play, and structured experiences. These are media through which children express their ideas to others. At learning centers children are free to "try out" a variety of ways to accomplish a task and are asked which way they prefer and why. These centers are facilitated not only to inform, but also to challenge critical thinking, imagination, creativity, inventiveness, and resourcefulness. A variety of procedures are employed throughout the day in exploration of open-ended relevant themes.

At CRE-ACT, rather advanced opportunities for children this young to "try out" their speaking ability are provided in the Elementary Speech Festival and the All School Dramatic Production which are held each year. Both of these are an integral part of the CRE-ACT program.

As classes in the Tryout Room begin, the first topic of the day may be to continue the discussion begun at Assembly in the morning. In an attempt to make the specific application more understandable to these young children, the teacher might suggest or solicit from the children a single appropriate practice on which the entire class will focus. In time, students will proudly recognize and point out other related responses not discussed in the assembly group. In the course of the day, children rotate in separate groups from one learning activity to another, each of which promotes acquisition of a different skill or experience. Some of these skills are essentially active and invite physical participation, while others are by nature mental and require that other stimuli be supplied for becoming constructively active. For this reason, children are encouraged to use their bodies to shape the forms of letters, become objects with specific sounds, and vocalize expressions before committing them to paper or a concrete shape.

A prime example is the alphabet. Many children can recite the letters routinely when they enter school, or even "chant" them proudly, "Now I know my ABC's!" But do they really "know" them? Children may be encouraged to make the A shape with their body.

> A is a tent with a little top floor
> It could hold two or three little people or more.

By spreading their feet apart and putting their arm or arms across below the knees, they can think A in another way. Next they are asked how many ways they can make the A shape with their hands, by using their fingers. This was by themselves, now how many ways can they make the single A shape with two other persons? Three? Five? Eight?

> B is a snowman, half in the sun.
> With half of him gone he's half as much fun!

With the next letter the children make the shape with their own body, bending one arm and leg on the same side. Can they make it with their hands only? With two other children? Six? Can they think of anything else having this shape? Who or what can they name that begins with this sound? Can they act it out for others to observe and guess? Procedures like these involve much more of the student than reciting from memory or making a form on paper. They proceed from working/thinking alone to interacting with others, planning and problem solving imaginatively.

Poetry and literature are introduced not only in their original form, but also as raw material for creative development. The nursery rhymes and stories wait to be infused with delightful creative alternatives for enjoyment. Consider, for example, the poem, *Little Miss Muffet*. The teacher asks participants to sit in a circle. One student enters the circle as Miss Muffett. Another, the spider, finds an appropriate position. Those forming the circle recite the poem. During this recitation the characters act. After the poem is enacted in its original form, children suggest alternative situations for the characters. Where else might Miss Muffet be? What/who else might come to her? Does everything have to frighten her? What else might she be eating or doing? Before this single work of literature is exhausted, every student has had an opportunity to suggest and enact several roles, and interact with the entire class.

At the Arts Center children will often in some way "sign" their work with their manner of expression. In an art composition of appropriate food for a meal, size and color intensity may reveal what a child's taste buds relish. Foods that they particularly favor are usually a bit exaggerated in size. The manner in which students combine fruit and vegetable shapes to make jewelry or print gift wrap, may reveal a kind of food they would like to share with others. Children are delighted when they have an opportunity to cook and enjoy their "homemade" bread, butter, 'stone' soup or snacks, not only by eating these foods themselves, but learning to serve them to other children. Math activities incorporate the actual measuring of ingredients needed for food preparation,determining basic money values for purchasing foods, and employing simple measuring units. Such integration of all aspects of the curriculum to bear on a single theme is a key to intense learning. Visits to the farm, the zoo, the greenhouse, or other sources of first hand information are an integral part of science units.

In addition to dramatizing stages in life cycles of plants and animals, a normal conclusion of a study often includes the enactment called "the part and the whole." One student begins by taking the shape of a part of a creature and announcing, for example, "I am the antenna of a butterfly." Another follows, "I am the head of the butterfly". The sequence of building requires that the one continuing to build becomes the base of the preceding part, or at least connected to what was previously constructed. Once the shape is begun, the process of building cannot be interrupted by another part starting in isolation from the others. So the next part in this example must become the body, or an eye or some other organ in the head, and so the butterfly takes shape. When completed, the unified "animal"ty performs actions directed by the initiator. Other types of beginnings might be, "I am the cat's ear," "I am the lightening in a storm cloud," or "I am the tulip bulb in the flower bed." This process has the potential to be a model for the study of community.

There are many ways in which other curricular content themes might be developed, incorporating dramatic expression. While decorating their own cowboy or cowgirl hats, as part of a Western unit, children choose from feathers, buttons, yarn, ribbon, pins, beads, buckles, etc. There are never two completed products alike. Sporting hats and a kerchief around their neck, they mount their imaginary steeds and head for the rodeo. After this, related questions are posed: What else might you lasso? Besides lassoing for fun, how else might one use a lasso? Typical responses might include rescuing someone or something from a river, or bringing down a kite caught in a tree.

On the average of once every other week, the students from one of the older grades join with the kindergarteners. The older student invites one or more of the little ones to a comfortable "nook" in the hallway or another space to read aloud to them. The younger ones are encouraged to ask questions or make comments. Older students pride themselves when this occurs. Many positive relationships develop as a result.

Leaving the self-contained Tryout Space, consideration will now be given to the Curricular Designated Classroom Spaces.

The Script Room

Whole Language Arts Space

> "In the beginning was man . . . but man, in one important way, was different. He spoke—and the universe listened. What did he say? How did he say it? No one knows . . . But the word came, and with it came thought, and then there was language, building bridges from man to man, from past to present, from present to future, from earth to heaven"[4]
>
> Editors of READ Magazine, *"Words, Words, Words"*

Language, as a medium of expression, is developed first as an aspect of curriculum in its own right, and then as a form/tool of other curricular content areas to convey additional meaning.

Language is concerned with the manner in which a creature expresses itself. Whether that creature is a bird, an animal, an insect, or a human being, the sounds it makes become one way in which it can make itself known. This is why language is thought of primarily as speech, talking, conversing, or word of mouth. But there are other ways of communication. One's pace and manner of walking frequently bespeak age, position of authority, or emotional attitude. The very direction and manner in which one moves, may express fear, anxiety, frustration, or elation. At times like this, the "body" is talking without the use of language. And then there are times when the real message is concealed by a non-commital response such as silence, laughter, or grimace. Of these three ways of expressing language, the first is the most generally recognized. When the language is one which is common or peculiar to the people of a race or nation, communication, the spoken word, is more easily understood. At CRE-ACT, however, the creative dramatics dimension includes all three. Words, no matter how many there are, are thought of merely as symbols, and can be interpreted in various ways. Therefore, the importance of body involvement will always be stressed.

A word familiar to even the very young is "stop." It may have been one of the first words children learned to read when riding in a car. Vocally, they have heard it time and again, asking them to discontinue an action in which they are engaged. As a way of experiencing the word physically, students are invited to stand in a circle. The leader, standing inside the circle, directs:

Tell me "stop"
    —with the palm of your hand

—with your foot
    . . . another way with your foot
        . . . still another way with your foot
(Participants will discover the potential of changing whole
body position such as sitting down or facing backward in
the process)
—with your elbow
—with your eyes
—with your whole body because you are scared
    . . . because you are angry
    . . . because you are annoyed
    . . . because you are uncertain
    . . . because you want to talk to them

As a buildup to total body involvement, the leader may direct, "Imagine now that you have left the house and are crossing a busy street. You don't notice until you are almost across it that your dog got out of the house and is following you. There is danger that your dog will be killed by oncoming traffic. How will you stop the oncoming cars? Use your whole body including your voice!" From the very beginning of this exercise, in order to make sure that participants really experience the word, the leader "tests" or attempts not to "stop" until adequate resistance is felt. Through physical experience students become aware that a single word may have different connotations, depending on the context in which it is used.

Word awareness is enriched through the development of synonyms. Participants are invited to move to one end of the classroom, allowing space for movement to the opposite end as the leader invites them one by one to "come." No repetition is allowed in the manner of "coming." As each skips, creeps, stomps, etc., students name the synonym for "come" which is written on the chalkboard. Shyness or indifference begins to disappear as the stockpile of more common synonyms are used. After each has had an opportunity, there is an audible gasp as the leader moves to the opposite end of the room and repeats, "Come." By this time students volunteer, as they are ready. If the challenge is too difficult, assistance in the form of, "How did you feel when. . . .?" might be offered, or another student with an idea might share and the two come as a couple. It is only toward the end of this activity that the more unusual words appear. Creativity results only from pushing beyond the ordinary into the unfamiliar space. Second graders have discovered words such as "slithered" and "catapulted" during an average class period.

Activities such as these bear fruit in the creative writing exercises that follow. In their written compositions, students are required to choose a specific number of words from the list on the chalkboard, and may not use the words *come* or *came*. As they advance in the study of language arts, more creative forms of expression as well as parallel forms of expression are expected. The latter might include changing the setting (time or place), adding or subtracting a character in the plot, changing the ending or climax of the presentation. Similes and metaphors enliven book reports and in announcements for television, thus utilizing the mechanics of language through this whole person involvement. Relationships are evoked through impersonation and comparison. Who is a King Arthur today? An Albert Einstein? Or through an announcement such as:

> WANTED! A Big Bad Wolf who is eating pigs!
> REWARD: $900 Billion
> GO to: w.w.w.wolf.com.

The basic work in the Whole Language Classroom carries over into all other phases of the curriculum.

Company Costume

The Social Studies Space

> "We hold that the people—all the people—are endowed with certain inalienable rights, that among these are life, liberty, and the pursuit of happiness That to secure these rights, governments are instituted among men, deriving their just powers from the consent of the governed."[5]

> Editors of READ Magazine, *The American Dream*

Social Studies are the family customs that have become the costumes of the ages. Each aspect of heritage is replete with manifold types of characterization which assume their identity through the attire that is worn. Although costumes are not an essential for performance, they do have the potential and the power to "spark" the imagination and prompt the physical body to "take shape," thus helping the actor to take on and enact the role or character being performed. The students, no matter what religious, racial or national background, interact with what it has meant through the ages to be kings and queens, heroes and villains, saints and sinners. In order to discern the differences, they must recognize that both good and evil have characterized the human family from the beginning. That is why great writers remind us:

> "Lives of great men all remind us,
> We can make our lives sublime

And departing leave behind us,
Footprints on the sands of time."[6]

Henry W. Longfellow, *A Psalm of Life*

At the same time that a costume makes an impact on the actor, it is a tremendous asset to assist the audience to know when and where "they are going" in order to put their experience into context.

The scope and range of the Social Studies space includes more than history. One's identity takes form not only from personal interaction, but also from the non-personal interaction with environments—the places, geographic conditions, political/civic organizations, and cultural influences that have an impact on our lives. All these, as well as personal interactions, become part of the colorful hue and texture, the warp and woof that designs the costume of mankind throughout the ages.

Family history at the kindergarten level focuses on the child's physical characteristics and membership in the immediate family. In the lower elementary grades, the focus is on the child's place in the extended family. Through study and field trips to community and civic organizations, an expanded concept of family is established. After visiting the Fire Department, the Post Office, Public Utilities, Law Enforcement, Medical Center, etc., the children organize their own classroom community model. Areas of responsibility for each person are identified and problems referred to the proper department: "Speeding" tickets are issued for running in the building or not waiting one's turn in line. Lunch bags/snacks found on the playground are referred to "garbage collectors." Victims of scrapes and bruises are brought to the "school nurse." Messages are delivered to the "post office" or "broadcasting system." etc. Council meetings are held to promote understandings and clear up difficulties. Organization of this nature allows students to act, to perform in real life situations, and to come to a better understanding of the extended family, their community.

The concept of extended family takes itself to the state level, beginning with grade four. After a variety of ways of gathering information have been learned through the computer, reading, field trips to government offices and buildings, visits from pioneers and natives within the United States, students are ready to dramatize their understanding of their state's history. For this activity, students arrange themselves to form the outline shape of the state which is being considered. In this instance it is the state of Idaho. The space cleared is approximately half of a large classroom, depending on the size of the class. State boundaries are identified by individual students representing specific neighboring states and locating. themselves accordingly. One by one they identify themselves in order to clarify the location of Idaho, its people, product, or occupation. For example, a bear or form of wild life could represent Montana; a bucking bronco, Wyoming; abeehive, Utah; and an apple picker, Washington. For Oregon, a student might fell a tree, calling, "TIMBER!" The next step in the process is the formation of the terrain of the state: flat desert in the south, buttes and plateaus in the central region, and rugged mountains in the north. Gestures, posture, and the reach of a student's body will indicate the type of terrain. Another student impersonates the Snake River, "snaking" its way from Yellowstone National Park in the northeastern region to the Columbia River in the Northwest. Major cities are likewise represented bodily according to their best known product or reason for growth. Blackfoot, Idaho, for example, is known as the potato center of the world. Pocatello was an Indian chief at Fort Hall, which is presently at the outskirts of the city that bears his name. Boise is the capital of the state, so the Capitol building is the basis of representation. Students must creatively consider how they will image these cities so that all will grasp the configuration. Further historical details are included;e.g., fur trade, exchange with the natives, silver mining, explorations of Lewis and Clark raising of crops, recreational areas and sports.

Students need to become acquainted with their ancestors so that they appreciate more deeply the heritage that is theirs. This is particularly true for the upper elementary age students. After researching the national and state "halls of fame," they can boast of ancestry with persons such as Frank Church, at his time the youngest senator in Washington D.C.; Philo T. Farnsworth, the "Father" and inventor of television; J. R. Simplot, who started the potato empire of our nation; Harmon Kilibrew, who was second only to Babe Ruth in the American league; and Carole Farly who became the youngest leading soprano in Cologne Opera. Students dressed in costume present through story telling, improvisation, or enactment in some form an episode in the life of the historical figure that they have chosen. They may use props, photos, products, or examples of instruments/tools used by their predecessor. There is hardly a unit of social studies which cannot be developed meaningfully as long as the physical, mental, and creative resources of the students are integrated into a common effort.

Back Stage

The Science Space

> "The birds in the sky and the wind in the grass told us the earth was our gift from the Father and it belongs to all."[7]

Shoshoni proverb, *Sage Smoke*

How many times one sits in an audience and tries to figure out what was done backstage to create a spectacular rapid transformation. There is always an eagerness to know what is behind a closed door, in a locked box, in a wrapped gift. The "concealed" holds an aura of mystery. There is an anxiety to "see." Vision is the principal sense employed in comprehending the world around us. Seventy percent of a person's sense perceptors are located in the eyes. The media capitalizes on this premise in its use of television, newspapers, and billboards. Splashes of color, graphics, and exaggerations are employed to attract attention. Breakfast cereal boxes and the comics do this well.

Children get excited about something they find and call out, "Come and see!" A standard expression for proving a point has come to be, "Seeing is believing." The planetary eye, the Explorer, encircling the earth, has become a symbol of the need to search and research, to discover and become familiar with the basic scientific forces touching our lives.

The scientific world holds immeasurable areas of space to be discovered, mysteries that telescopes, microscopes and research have not touched. The eye, however, is not the only vehicle for obtaining insight. Touch, sound, movement, and whole-body involvement reveal new avenues for "looking into" spaces not yet explored. A creative dramatics approach incorporates and employs many of these facets simultaneously.

Visualizing as a means of learning, the focus for the lower elementary age is on what one can see naturally and to see these things as being stabilized— i.e., centered. The children observe sunrise and sunset, light and darkness, day and night, in a variety of cyclic modes. They see time being measured by clocks and calendars. As a way of helping children to see how this happens, the teacher or leader introduces the globe, our planet Earth, emphasizing its circular shape. Then children form a circle, facing the inside. Each, hands on hips,becomes the world with Pocatello (or some other fixed location) on the front. The teacher, in the center of the circle is the sun and asks, "What time of day is it when the sun shines directly on us? If this is noon, where is Pocatello at midnight?" (Students turn their backs to the sun.) "At sunrise? " (6 a.m.) "At sunset?" (6 p.m.) And so the concept of rotation as the basis for telling time is clarified. The concept of rotation may be further developed by having students take the shape of objects that rotate such as egg beaters, helicopters, windmills, videotapes, wheels of all kinds.

Making the distinction between rotation and revolution prepares the way for dramatizing the phases of the moon which in turn explains the basis for the division of time into weeks and months. A group of children gathered in the center of a circle represent the people on the earth. A child at a distance, draped in a yellow scarf becomes the sun, while another with a scarf covering the half of the body facing the sun, becomes the moon. As the moon revolves around the earth, always with the same side reflecting the sun's rays, the earth people perceive the moon in its phases, and the amount of time required to revolve once around the earth gives the basis for measurement of four weeks and a month.

Likewise, the reasons for the seasons can be enacted. If students are trained to be observant to the world about them, many of the laws governing the world of nature can be enacted. Ordinarily, the phrase, "going in circles" is deemed derogatory and imparts the meaning of getting nowhere. Perhaps this cliché needs to be re-examined, at least as one becomes more observant from a scientific viewpoint.

At the middle elementary age the emphasis shifts to gaining scientific insights requiring the use of instruments which aid the human eye. These include maps, diagrams, graphs, magnifying glasses, overhead projectors, microscopes and telescopes. Because maps are diagrams corresponding to a larger reality, they help to envision what one cannot see all at once. In this context it is possible to enact the manner in which the world is symbolically divided. A circle is the formation taken by a class to represent the world. Some students will join together to become the equator from which other lines of latitude are measured to the North and to the South. From these the surface is divided into zones and their climatic differences discussed and enacted. Lines of longitude, beginning with the Prime Meridian and including the International Dateline are established. Their use as guides in establishing time zones of the world may be pointed out. After this experience students are prepared to interpret the guidelines of longitude and latitude on maps, and with the assistance of the map legend, locate specific natural regions, cities, or other places of interest. These skills also help students to construct graphs and diagrams to interpret their own statistics in other subject areas, especially math. Microscopes and telescopes assist students to visualize objects otherwise not discernable to the human eye. Because they are too small or too distant for more than one or a few students to see at a time, dramatization of what is observed on a small scale can be an effective medium for sharing in a group context.

Students in the upper grades are challenged to experiment, to look beyond, to gain new "insights", and to uncover/discover information. Their research, to begin with, should be "centered" around a known or proven reality to give it a credible base from which to begin. The following potential areas of investigation require research on one's own, gathering information from interviews, recording, tabulating, and analyzing the data in order to arrive at a conclusion/solution.

1. What pollutants are found in the air in Bannock and Power Counties? Which geographical areas are most affected or infected? Are rural populations affected as much as the urban?
2. Devise a method of communicating quantity without using any known number system.
3. How do students at CRE-ACT School respond to specific colors? Is there a significant difference between the responses of younger and older children?
4. Compare the earth to a space ship—or to a merry-go-round.
5. Show how you think gravity would feel, look, and act if it were an animal, a machine or a person.
6. Dramatize what a satellite might think as it orbits the earth, as it goes over CRE-ACT School, or as it slows down about to re-enter the earth's atmosphere.

Sharing the information with others could take the form of public speaking, a demonstration, a newscast, an original play script, a parody, or any other dramatic form.

Students need time to think about what they are doing and why they are doing it. It is important to allow children time to respond to a question, especially if it is not the one on which they had focused. Different ways of thinking and responding may uncover insights other than the one on which the research focused. This makes the final report a critical part of the process.

Exploration is an investigation of the world. It is looking at new things and new places. It is also seeing the old in new ways. Exploration can be active, playful, dynamic. While some people explore distant lands and galaxies, others explore their own back yards. We are all explorers. Invite a child to accompany you as your guide.

The Scene Changing Room

The Mathematics Space

> "Life has many angles, dimensions, and proportions. It may appear abstract. We become fractional individuals when time is always a problem to solve. How much energy is expended in multiplying what is considered valuable? How much is divided with others? From the total added to those seemingly important things, how much is subtracted and given away? Life is about finite numbers . . . There are a finite number of times that we can add something of real worth to another person's life."[8]

> D. Frank McClane, *Monsters of mathematics*

Science heightens the consciousness of the world around us in terms of distance and space, revealing entities that are too small or too far away to be viewed by the naked eye. At the same time, math introduces the challenge of finding ways of measuring distance, time, size, quantity or value of these realities. How does one describe their presence or existence in relation to other elements? A number, the basic unit of measurement, is symbolic and abstract. Our technical computerized world has devised a digital base with a potential for attaching values ranging from the miniscule to the unimaginable—infinity. Until a base for concretizing these values is established, it is impossible for the mind to understand them. How can we build a bridge between these two worlds, the concrete and symbolic/abstract? How do we extend the particular to the general?

Some basic general standards for computation have already been established for general use: Cuisenaire rods, place value cubes, charts, graphs, rulers, compasses, and calculators, assist to a degree, but they are not enough. Students need to assume an active role in constructing mathematical meaning for themselves from within by ordering their perceptions and experiences into formats of their own.

The task of the math space is to define such areas for performance, furnishing them with or making available stimuli (props, tools, and raw materials) that will invite, attract attention, and focus the students' energies to achieve a specific end in view. Within these scenarios, students become actively involved with one another, with adults, and with materials that are concrete, real, and relevant to them.

The classroom "stage manager" must be extremely observant of each student's progress in order to know when and how to make scene changes that will insure appropriate environments, including props, to evoke and support the wide range and intensity of each student.

At this step in the process, the boundaries of the stage may "disappear," and the space become as long and wide, high and deep as the imaginations and creativity of the students extend it.

Numbers are the building blocks of mathematics. Number sense is a feel for the size, and meaning of numbers, the relationships between numbers, the way they can be put together and taken apart, and the connections between numbers and the world around us. One way of instilling this sense is to give students scenarios in which the numbers have been removed and listed separately. They must choose the proper associations. An example might be:

Numbers 610, 5, 75, and 10

Janna is <BLANK> feet tall and weighs <BLANK> pounds. Every day she rides her bike <BLANK> minutes to get to school. She lives at <BLANK> Maple Avenue.

When students are more at ease with number sense, they might write their own examples, careful to observe that each number fits only one blank.

Number/Could be/Couldn't be
10/# of bowling pins/# of bowling balls
28/# of teeth in a mouth/the number of times I brush my teeth each day.
40/# of pounds a dog weighs/the age of the dog

Number is an abstraction. Through experience students learn that a number must correspond to a quantity of things. They can eventually manipulate numbers as they manipulate blocks, regrouping them as needed (e.g., "carrying" in addition, "borrowing" in subtraction, etc.). The use of manipulative objects is similar to acting out problems. Physical actions with physical objects embody and give meaning to words and concepts like "divide", "half", "hundredths", etc.

Number sense finds its application in daily life; e.g. telling time, telling age, measuring height and weight, noting temperature, reading maps, telling distances, buying food, telling the date, etc. The first of these, telling time, plays a dominant role in our lives. In the normal course of the day how often one hears: "When do we eat? You'll miss the bus! You'll be late for your meeting. When will we get there? How many days before report cards come out? How many days before Christmas?"

Making clocks on paper plates with moving hands is a good practice, but it is not sufficient. It is much more effective to experience time physically. After all, it is the body that needs to be in a specific place at a specific time. Groups of 13 or 26 can play the following exercise at a time. Twelve children stand in a circle to form the clock face, each wearing a large clock number on a card around his/her neck. All face the center of the circle. A thirteenth person, the cuckoo, moves to the center of the circle, holding two dangling cords, one black to represent the hour hand, and one red for the minute hand. The leader calls a time such as five o'clock. "5" dashes to the center to grab the black "hour hand" cord, while "12 races for the red "minute hand" cord. They return quickly with their cords to their positions in the circle.

When the player in the center feels the cords are taut and the "hands" the correct ones, he calls out "cuckoo." If the leader calls, "ten after one", the players holding "1" and "2" race for the cords. But if the leader calls "half past six", one player, "6" would race for both cords, but hold the hour cord in the hand closer to the circle and the minute cord in his outside hand. When the children really know how to tell time, they can enact time problems such as, "It takes 20 minutes for Jane to get to school. She leaves home at eight o'clock. What time does she get to school?"

Making a time line is a way of recording not only the passage of time, but associating the development of a concept or a pattern of growth within it. Some topics for recording in this manner might be: the average life span of animals raised as family pets, time required to prepare foods, ages of family members, times and places of vacation travel, political leaders of a geographical area during a specific period of history, etc.

One of the most enjoyable phases of defining space is associated with physical enacting of geometric shapes. In a cleared space providing at least a 6 foot area for each person, the leader gives directions such as:

Make a vertical line with your finger, with your hand, with your arm, with your whole body.

Make a horizontal line with your fingers, your hand, your arm, with both arms, with your leg.

Make an oblique line with your leg, with your finger, with your arm, with your body above the hips, with both legs.

Form a perpendicular with your fingers, with your hands, your arms, your feet, legs.

Form a right angle with your fingers, your hands,, your arms, your feet, your legs, with another part of your body.

Form an obtuse angle with your head and one arm.

Form parallel lines with your hands, your fingers.

Now with these basic forms, how many right triangles can you form with your whole body at one time?

Other geometric shapes such as rectangles, obtuse triangles, isosceles triangles, trapezoids, can be drawn on the board or large pieces of paper laid on the floor. These could form the basis for problem solving, designing art murals, or stage sets and props.

When it comes to problem solving, students often find adventure in the process. They represent a problem using drawings, or enact the process of a problem by using objects to act out the problem themselves. This again reinforces the connection between ideas regarding the solution of a problem and the real-world possibility of solutions.

The Dressing and Make-up Room

The Religion Space

"A moral map is indispensable for determining the boundaries of human behavior. The distance between right and wrong is measured. Significant paths to take are marked. The contours, direction of currents, and depth soundings in life are charted ."[9]

D. Frank McLane, *Should've Been a Cowboy*

Because The Franciscan CRE-ACT School is a Roman Catholic entity, it is the Catholic faith that is presented in Religion class and is integrated into the other aspects of the school day. The curriculum provides for an understanding of faith in practice consonant with that of the elementary school child. As explained previously, several different faiths are represented in the student body. In keeping with CRE-ACT's practice of providing a wide range of opportunity for its students, all attend religion class and participate according to their ability, but no attempt is made to convert anyone or to coerce them to embrace the Roman Catholic faith. Should such a desire be expressed, the matter is pursued with the parents of the student.

Imitation is a powerful tool in dramatic education. At a very young age, children love to "dress up" in trailing skirts, high heels, hats that slip over their eyes, and shirts whose cuffs reach their ankles. It isn't the appearance that counts, but the internal "boost" the spirit gets for growth from an experience which would never happen without the charm of pretense, of imitation, which dressing up affords. A comparable energy comes from putting on make-up, a mask that frees the child to try on a personality other than the self. This dramatic stimulus stays with us throughout our lives. Every time a student is cast in a dramatic production, another opportunity presents itself to try on and experience life from another viewpoint.

Nowhere does this become more challenging than in Religion class when students are encouraged to improve their behavior and become better persons. Christ and the saints become examples for them to imitate: "Learn from Me, for I am meek and humble of heart." Attempting to act in a specific manner is a way of "dressing up" to become like the model: "Put on the Lord Jesus Christ." The costume is worn until its likeness becomes integral to the person. Once these prototypes become part of a person's life, the student is encouraged to "try on" another exemplar. In this manner, the inner life of the spirit grows as well as the intellectual, physical, and emotional.

In practice, the chief exemplar to present to the students for imitation is Jesus Christ Himself who, although He was God, became a human being in order to show us the way in which to live: "I am the Way, the Truth, and the Life." Presenting as a model one of their own chronological age to begin with gives the students a head start with one basis of similarity. The choice of obedience as a focal point puts the challenge in a perspective required of all persons. It will not be difficult for children to conclude that obedience was not always easy, even for Jesus. Because He was both God and man, He had knowledge of circumstances far surpassing that of His parents or elders, yet He submitted and obeyed. Points for discussion might include:

1. Obedience to parents—Jesus left the learned men in the temple and came back to Nazareth as requested by His parents.
2. Obedience to civil authority—payment of the taxes.
3. Obedience to His heavenly Father—the pain and suffering of His passion and death on the cross: "My God, My God, why have you forsaken Me?

St. Nicholas, a model of generosity, often gets "lost" in the materialistic emphasis of the Christmas season. Holding a St. Nicholas Day celebration provides an opportunity for students to get acquainted with this saint who secretly shared his possessions with the needy and unfortunate. Students craft Christmas decorations and gifts to share with persons in unfortunate situations. They also draw names of other children in the school to whom they become "secret angels" and for whom they perform kind deeds or leave tokens affirming their new friend in some way.

Mother Teresa of Calcutta is a modern apostle whose playful wit strikes right to the heart of situations that frequently don't seem to make sense, and often puts children in awkward positions. Some of her maxims include:

1. If you are honest and frank, people may cheat you. Be honest and frank anyway.
2. What you spend years building, someone could destroy overnight. Build anyway.
3. The good you do today, people will often forget tomorrow. Do good anyway.
4. Give the world the best you have, and it may never be enough. Give the world the best you have anyway.[10]

These proposals for models who might serve as inspirations to the students are merely suggestions. The instructor has to become aware of individual and group needs as they arise and the potential of the students to respond to the model or models at the time.

The Warm-up Room

The Physical Education Space

"Every man is the builder of a temple called his body . . . We are all sculptors and painters, and our material is our own flesh and blood and bones. Any nobleness begins at once to refine a man's feature, any meanness or sensuality to imbrute them."[11]

Henry David Thoreau, *Light From Many Lamps*

Just as carpenters sharpen their tools, farmers oil their machines, baseball pitchers "wind up," and musicians "tune up," so the human body needs frequent "servicing" in order to maintain quality performance. It is beneficial to recall from time to time that the physical body experiences fatigue and may need "refueling" in order to meet your expectations of it. As the physical muscles are toned, so too the psychological, social, attitudinal, and creative aspects of personhood are reinvigorated and brought into association with one another. Physical education class has a unique potential for calling forth and revealing aspects of personhood frequently unnoticed or untapped. One's true person becomes more visible. Because of the wide range of skills tapped, it is nearly impossible to excel in everything. Sounds ranging from tears to fears, anxieties, and hurrahs are not uncommon.

Physical education serves as a medium for the student to become more conscious of, sort out, and inter-relate personal resources and abilities. Re-entering the classroom routine might be compared to a spaceship re-entering Earth after viewing oneself and one's world from a new perspective after "discovering" and "warming up" to whom one more realistically is.

The "key note" to the activities which follow is that all students are involved at all times.

Ghost Tag

Preparation: Students are each given a clean, empty gallon size plastic bottle. They are instructed to decorate the bottle using permanent magic markers. A theme focusing on artistic expression might be suggested.

Game: Students take their decorated bottle and a small ball {such as a tennis ball) out to a space on the playing field. Each student protects the bottle without touching it, simultaneously using the ball to knock down other bottles. In order that all students be involved at all times, the game is conducted so that when a bottle is knocked down the owner must take the bottle to a new space on the field and resume playing from there. This also alleviates the problem of certain students ganging up on another student to get a certain one out; this game builds unity and community involvement.

Dodge Ball (non-traditional)

Students are placed in groups of three. Each group is given a ball. The object is to bounce the ball between two players at the feet of the third player and try to get the player "out" by "hitting" him with the ball. When the player is "hit," instead of leaving the game, the student trades places with the player who threw the ball and play resumes.

True/False Tag (Great for any subject integration)

Two teams, "Trues" and "Falses" face off in the middle of a field or gym area with a safety area behind for each team. The teacher makes a statement. If it is correct, "Trues" chase "Falses". If incorrect, "Falses" chase "Trues." Anyone caught becomes a member of the other team.

The Part and the Whole

One of the major goals in health education should be to develop an awareness and appreciation of the human body. One of the quickest ways of accomplishing this is to single out the various parts of the body, compare them with an object or instrument with which the students are already familiar, and have them enact it. The following are some suggestions:[12]

The Brain
    computer
    filing cabinet
The Eyes
    cameras
The Ears
    drum
    anvil
The Nose
    filters
    strainers
    vacuum cleaners
The Teeth
    knives
    grinders
The Voice
    Stringed instruments
The Lungs
    Balloons
    Bellows
The Kidneys
    Filter system
The Tendons
    suspension bridge
    cables

The Muscles
    sun-powered engines
    elastic
The Blood
    red cells—construction workers
    white cells—health department
    blood platelets—seamstresses
The Nerves
    computer networks
    telegraphic system
The Joints
    hinges
    ball and socket
The Heart
    pump
    pipes
    valves
The Stomach
    factory
    refinery
The Intestines
    garbage disposal
The Arch
    bridge

Even with the most simplistic activity, a hero can emerge when physical education is used to promote unity rather than competition. One afternoon the first and second graders finished P.E. with an exercise in shooting basket balls. The smallest student (who is very sensitive about his height) made the first basket. The whole class cheered for him each time it was his turn. He succeeded three times to make a basket. It was evident from his spirited sharing with faculty and older students that he "grew" that day.

ARTS RELATED AREAS

"During the past quarter century, literally thousands of school-based programs have demonstrated beyond question that the arts can not only bring coherence to our fragmented academic world, but through the arts, students' performance in other academic disciplines can be enhanced as well"[13]

Ernest Boyer, *For the Advancement of Teaching.*

Expressive Movement

The Dance Space Room

" . . . dancing is imperatively needed to give poise to the nerves, schooling to the emotions, strength to the will, and to harmonize the feelings and the intellect with the body which supports them."[14]

Stanley Hall

Movement and body language are the predominant means of communication between people. The very young express most things through movement whether it be discomfort, pleasure, joy, or fear. As people grow older, social pressures and expectations inhibit this freedom to be spontaneous and creative. Dance becomes an effective learning tool because the student becomes aware of the body as a physical, emotional and cognitive instrument connecting action, feeling and thought. Dance expands the student's physical image by encouraging the use of familiar movements in new ways. This requires physical and emotional risk taking. Group activities offer experiences in collaboration, trust and ensemble work. Ideas and feelings that are difficult to express in words can be explored and conveyed through movement imagery, either negating or reinforcing spoken language of its own.

Because special skills are not pre-requisites, students not previously trained in dance can expand their understanding of factual subject matter through kinesthetic experiences. Skills are discovered through individual and collaborative expressions. Expressive movement is predominantly improvisational (creation and execution take place simultaneously). It can include dramatization, symbolization, characterization and impression. But its mode is always physical. It is the body and the body's movement that communicate the story, the idea, the poem, the atmosphere, the statement, or the emotion. During the stage in which movements are being explored and "tried out" or "tried on" by a participant, they are not meant for the entertainment of an audience. Once they have been rehearsed adequately, they can be shared and enjoyed by both. It is CRE-ACT's belief that no education is complete without this type of experience. Dance is perhaps the easiest of the arts with which to integrate other curricular areas. There are so many ways in which movement can be used that it allows other ideas to be easily explored.

Basic Movements

A good starting point, generally, for younger children or anyone lacking experience in this art, is to explore first the potential of basic body movements to convey a thought or message. Positioning participants in circular formation and engaging all in the same directive at the same time helps to give participants a sense of security, of belonging. As self-confidence grows, and participants need more room to implement their movements, they might be directed to find their own space, which extends approximately a yard around them. Directions then include an action in relation to something:
    For hands and arms:

REACH for an apple; to unscrew a light bulb; to get a book from a high shelf; to catch a base ball; for a coin you dropped.
STRETCH to look over a tall fence, to jump across a stream; to shoot a bow and arrow; a glove to fit your hand.
PULL a carrot from the garden; the rope for water skiing; the peeling from a banana; the water hose; the bell rope.
LIFT a large watermelon; a heavy box of books; a small child who has fallen; a rosebud to smell it.
PICK UP an ear of corn; a football; a marshmallow; a donut; the saddle for a horse; a glass you broke.

In a follow-up phase of movement exploration the director names an action and asks the students individually to identify the recipient of or place of the action:

For leg and foot movement:
    stamping, tip toeing, bending, clicking heels, sliding
Ways to move:
    under, backward, sideways, beneath, over

Directions in which to move:
Up, down, backward, forward, over, under, between, across.

Several such actions may be enacted in succession to a musical melody to create a dance pattern.
Simple poetry also provides the stimulus for basic body awareness.

> Jump or Jiggle
> Frogs jump.
> Caterpillars hump.
> Worms wiggle.
> Bugs jiggle.
> Rabbits hop.
> Horses clop.
> Snakes slide.
> Seagulls glide.
> Mice creep.
> Deer leap.
> Puppies bounce.
> Lions stalk.
> But I walk.[15]
>
> Poetry Anthology

Individuality and Cooperation

Older students were encouraged to create an eight-count movement phrase that expressed their personality. After sharing their unique expressions individually, the participants executed their own movements all at the same time, being careful to establish pathways which would not interfere with each other. Then, with the assistance of the instructor, they created a movement phrase in which the entire class enacted in succession each student's movements, one following the other.. This exercise gave the students a chance to explore their individuality, realizing that it could exist while cooperating with others. It also was an opportunity to experience the need to set aside their specific individuality to work as a group in order to accomplish a specific goal.

Aspects of nature

Students were asked to think of different aspects of nature, especially natural phenomenon such as storms, geysers, volcanoes, tornadoes, etc. Standing in a circle, they improvised movements of 4, 8, or 16 counts that portrayed these elements. These were put in sequential order and performed to music by George Gershwin's "Drifting Along With the Tide." Students responded especially well to exploding like a volcano in the middle of a circle, then backing out like flowing lava, or the spiral movement of a tornado, drawing whatever is in its path into its central core.

Animals vs. Nature.

Students divided into two groups, one representing aspects of nature and one representing animals. Each group stood on opposite sides of the room facing each other. The nature group used movements to represent waves, wind, hail, etc., while the animal group used their characteristic actions such as creeping, crawling, or leaping movements. Two groups approached each other, the animals struggling to defend and protect themselves from the elements. Animals also explored ways of assisting one another to escape to safety, or to enjoy comradery in non-threatening situations.

The complementary patterns of movement expressive of offensive and defensive relationships have the potential of application to a wide range of curricular and behavioral themes such as war/peace, justice/injustice, darkness/light, hope/despair, joy/sorrow, life/death.

The Design Room

The Visual Arts Space

"The process of studying and creating art in all of its distinct forms defines those qualities that are at the heart of education reform—creativity, perseverance, a sense of standards, and above all a striving for excellence."[16]

Richard W. Riley

The role of visual art, like that of dance, is to take the student beyond the factual, in order to expand and explore the meaning of concepts. What dance accomplishes through movement, visual art accomplishes through imagery. While dance attempts to explore HOW something is, visual art examines WHAT something is. As the name implies, this is pursued through visual media such as drawings, paintings, photos, sculptures, carvings, tapestries— images that connote in some shape and form, a conception that an artist wishes to express. These might be crispness of snow, splendor of a sunrise, the mischief in a baby sister or brother, the message hidden in the wrinkles of an elderly person's face, or the despair in a refugee's countenance.

The challenge of the artist is to find the manner in which these images relate or can be brought into relationship with one another. What design/configuration do they make? What emotions do they arouse when placed in proximity with one another? Just as in dance and theatre the potential for further expression increases when an individual interacts in and with a group, so in art, each element enhances or is enhanced reciprocally, given its proper correlation. Each element has its own characteristics and identity that must be taken into consideration.

Each of us is a craftsman, entrusted with the task of designing our own life, of making it a work of art—a masterpiece. But it requires more than one element to make a design. The more varied the texture, hue, form and shape of media employed, the greater will be the possibility of finding new and striking designs in our world. Some ways in which the concept of design has been explored follow.

Design—animal footprints

After a series of classroom activities focusing on a unit about animals in winter, the preschool and kindergarten students went on a field trip to a nearby national forest where animal tracks were observed, measured and drawn. The students identified which animals created the tracks. In art class each child drew several animal tracks of their choice. These drawings were used to create their own individual stamps made from inner tube pieces glued to cardboard. The children inked these and stamped them on paper in such a way as to look as if an animal had just walked around on the page. Each child was encouraged to look closely at one print and to select a second distinct from the first to "walk on the page" with the other. Discussion followed:

Which tracks are larger?
How are they shaped differently?
Do they look good together?
Might they look better arranged in a crisscross or winding pattern?
Could your two animals get along well together?

Creating stories about why or why not these animals would be friends or enemies, and designing other groupings accordingly followed this discussion. Scenes showing changes in differing behavioral patterns were dramatized.

Design—Transportation models

During the study of a social studies theme of transportation at the intermediate level, students designed various modes of conveyance. They constructed two three-dimensional projects. The first used recycled materials including egg cartons, towel rolls, sponges, plastic pieces, spools, styrofoam, etc. Students chose different materials to represent various parts of their vehicles: a sponge ball for the top of a hot air balloon, a discarded plastic box for the body of a car, spools for wheels, rubber tubing over toilet paper rolls for the wheels on a show cart. Students interacted with adult volunteers and other students as they determined the best ways to display their work. They shared what they had learned and were better able to communicate this knowledge through their creations. Elements of design developed by students reflected their understanding of vehicle construction, their personal preferences, and artistic values. These models were displayed and discussed with the rest of the class after completion.

The second project utilized large cardboard boxes and paint. The students created vehicles in which they could ride, drive, or fly. Adults helped cut designs and holes large enough for the students to fit inside, but the students painted their own creations and added details. Creative Drama was used as students displayed or sold their vehicles at an "auction". Just as each vehicle was an element of design in itself, as the succession of vehicles moved along, prime prerogatives and special features of each such as size, speed, attractiveness, and purpose, were recognized. These formed other patterns and designs as a group. Discussion included: Could your vehicle be driven by anyone? Would it require special training to operate? Is it sports related? Can it transport heavy loads? Would it be safe for children? Where would it be used and for what purpose? The skill gained in this type of activity was a great asset in the construction of props and sets for the annual play productions.

Masks

All over the world, in theatre and dance, in religion and art, the mask has played a prominent part. While "trying on someone else" through the mask, one can feel free to be anyone or anything one would like to be. The youngest children enjoy cutting eyes, nose, and mouth in a paper bag and putting it over their heads. Gradually these bags become more ornate with additions or alterations. Social studies and literature provide many opportunities for making and using masks. The following became part of the Egyptian unit—to make a Pharaoh's mask.

Students began to build the form out of clay on a solid water-resistant base slab. The next step was to cover the model with paper mache' strips, making sure to use plenty of paste. The mask could not be removed from the form until it was completely dry. This provided time for planning color schemes, design, and impressions one wanted to convey. The masks were painted, shellacked, and became part of the presentation of an Egyptian Day Experience for parents, friends, and visitors. The skill also became an asset in making masks for dramatic productions.

Three-dimensional representations

During a study of dinosaurs students incorporated what they had read and seen to create clay dinosaurs. The challenge was to transform two-dimensional pictures and drawings into three- dimensional forms with correct proportions. Students investigated logical colors for their creatures and found that they had some freedom of interpretation in this area. This allowed for some color experimentation and composition discussion. Their completed dinosaurs were used in science class, discussed with other students and adults, and put on display.

The Sound Room

The Music Space

> "If art and music, color and design, and poetry were nothing more than decorative, both life and worship could be just as meaningful without them. But art opens up meaning, and opens us to its meaning. Music does more than enhance. . . . it exegetes, it interprets, and it is angelic. It carries words and messages to inner chambers of our souls for which only music has the key. Music has power to help us understand."[17]

Pastor W. Bruce Benson

Have you ever come to a point when you just couldn't find words to express what was in your heart or on your mind? Sometimes there just isn't appropriate diction to match the intensity one knows or feels at such times. Some writers coin their own words, but there is another form of expression which can go far beyond the literally concrete. Music has this potential. Whether accompanied by words or not, music has the power to express or convey a message—it speaks, and it speaks in terms of sound. While dance attempts to explore WHO something is, and visual art examines WHAT something is, music clarifies WHY something is. Musical expression is directly tied to interpretation. The performer has to try to understand what the composer is trying to communicate, and then tailor the performance to realize that intent. Interpretation requires an attention to detail. Performing music is not just a matter of getting the notes right; it is making every note mean something. Singing is sustained speech. The performer has to " phrase," that is, convey the logic of the melodic flow. All music breathes. There have to be resting points or places that mark the end of the phrase or musical thought. Just as there is a natural rise and fall in the way we speak a sentence, there is a rise and fall in the way we perform a musical phrase.

For music to communicate, it must be expressive. Each one brings to it personal talent, feeling and personality. But music also invites us to invent. This kind of spontaneous musical invention is called "composition." The improviser is simultaneously a composer and a performer.

I Have A Car

American Camp Song

Rain, Rain, Go Away

Traditional

See See

Children's Camp Song

Figure 9.1. Music

Music is one of the ways we define who we are as individuals and as a society. Although there are infinite varieties for infinite tastes, music itself is a universal language that communicates emotion and can transport the listener or performer to another place, or even a different time. Children learn by "doing" music as much as by thinking it. For many, to "do" music is to come to understand it, in that physical involvement provides a fuller intellectual and emotional experience.

Mechanical sounds

Music incorporating mechanical sounds conveys a message of its own. Even before becoming involved in music as such, children attribute a wide range of sounds to toy vehicles and machines as they play with them. The song "I have a Car"[18] (Music sheet 9.1) has been a medium for teaching musical concepts as well as making them meaningful. Students gain a better understanding of pitches and rhythms by singing and clapping the notes.

The rhythm found in words makes them more expressive. Two eighth notes taking the place of a quarter note give the impression of speeded up movement as exemplified in "Rain, Rain Go Away"[19] (Music Sheet 9.1). One hears the patter of single drops in the quarter notes, their going and coming in the eighth notes.

Another example can be seen in the Children's Camp Song, "See See"[20] (Music sheet 9.1).

In this notation, the length of the dotted half note conveys the message of a command as well as the theme; the half note the main concepts under consideration: horse and tail. Rhythm is part of life; producing and responding to rhythm opens the mind to much more than music. Learning to feel rhythm in music increases the ability to hear and understand rhythm in math, reading, and physiology, as well as throughout the man-made and natural world. To be able to move in rhythm with others allows children a way to bridge across our diverse world community of language and cultural differences.

Poetic accompaniment

Language, especially poetry with its meter and cadence, has the potential of inspiring musical accompaniment. In the book, *JOYFUL NOISE*, Paul Fleischman verbally recreates the booming, boisterous, joyful noise of insects. The poetry is written to be read aloud with two readers at once, one taking the left-hand part, the other the right hand part. As the poems are read from top to bottom, the two parts mesh in a musical duet. When both readers have lines at the same horizontal level, those lines are spoken simultaneously. The following arrangement was an excellent medium for introducing the students to "part" singing. It also encouraged students to compose their own musical accompaniment.

Fireflies

Light	Light
	is the ink we use.
Night	Night
is our parchment.	

We're
fireflies,

fireflies   flickering,
flitting,
                    flashing,

fireflies
glimmering,   fireflies
                    gleaming,
glowing
insect calligraphers   insect calligraphers,
practicing penmanship,
                    copying sentences,
six-legged scribblers   six-legged scribblers
of vanishing messages,
                    fleeting graffiti.[21]

Paul Fleischman, *Joyful Noise*

Musical instruments

Because the one instrument we always have is the voice, singing is the first focus of instruction. Learning songs that are part n of our national identity such as patriotic, folk, religious and popular gives the students an ability to be part of and sing within a larger community than just CRE-ACT.

The recorder is the primary instrument that is used to reinforce and solidify the concepts used in music. It is an accessible, easy to learn instrument that encourages self-awareness and fine motor skills for students third grade and above. Rhythm instruments (both pitched and non- pitched) are used extensively throughout the year and with all grades, starting with preschool. Violin and guitar instruction have also been a part of the program.

Kinesthetics

In addition to singing, rhythm and other instruments, the music program includes kinesthetic applications. By including dance and musical games, teamwork and group activities as well as individual skill development and dramatization of musical concepts and skills the whole person is being affected. Rhythm is part of life: producing and responding to rhythm opens the mind to much more than music. Learning to hear and feel rhythm in music increases the ability to hear and understand rhythm in reading, math, and science, as well as throughout the man-made and natural world. To be able to move in rhythm with others allows students a way to bridge across our diverse world community of language and cultural differences.

Arts Integrated Projects

Liturgical Celebration

In October and November, at the same time that the children learned a liturgical dance in dance class, they were learning methods of harvesting food in science class, and making preparations for a liturgical service in religion class. A strong correlation developed among these aspects of the curriculum, integrating art, religion, dance, music, art, social studies, and science. Students designed and created costumes, accessories, and hoops to be worn at this special event. Sashes and ties were measured and designed carefully so as not to hamper movement. The children chose seasonal colors common during harvest time (yellow, red, and dark brown). They also helped the teacher prepare three dye baths for soaking the fabric pieces. Paraffin wax was melted and old paintbrushes gathered for applying the wax to the fabric. Students decided what parts of their costumes should remain white and painted those areas with the wax. The garments were then placed in the lightest dye bath, yellow, to soak over night. The following day they were rinsed and hung to dry. During the next class a similar procedure was followed to establish a yellow area, which was covered with wax and placed in the red dye bath. Any area not previously covered with wax or newly covered, became brown in the last die bath. When the garments were completely dry, the students took turns ironing them between sheets of newspaper to remove the wax. While waiting to iron, the other students used batik scraps to decorate hoops for the dance.Care was taken to measure carefully to keep the hoops manageable and thus not hinder the dance. At the next rehearsal costumes and accessories were used and adjusted as necessary. Needless to say, the dance gave a distinct festive tone to the entire service. These creations became part of the CRE-ACT costume department and were used for years in numerous performances after. Students took pride in sharing their creations with others, and always associated them with what they had learned in art, science, math, dance, and religion.

Vegetable Prints

A series of vegetable prints were made by all the students in the school. These were created at the culmination of the harvest discussions, activities and a science field trip. Many examples of vegetables and fruits, including some from the field trip, were cut in different ways, examined and drawn from different points of view during the first art class. During the next class some of these same vegetables were dipped in colored ink or paint and printed on paper in patterns, spiral designs or representational compositions. Some were used to make greeting cards, place mats, paper tablecloths, and gift wrap. A display was arranged in the school's Prokes Art Gallery and later taken home.

Idaho History

An Idaho history activity completed by the fifth and sixth graders was used by all the students in the school. Idaho county maps were enlarged with the use of an overhead projector and transferred to press board. They were organized into a large floor puzzle map of Idaho. After painting the map, students added major features and each piece was covered with a clear protective coat. The map was ready to be used by the entire school. In addition to working on the puzzle during class times, the map was used by children of all age levels who arrived at school early before classes began.

Features

The School Community at Large

> "We want children to communicate. We want them, pari passu,to reveal their uniqueness by their works. For it is by their works—not their grades—that we shall know them. More important, it is by their works that they will know themselves. The schools need to become, not only places for equal opportunity, but for varied opportunity. We need, in effect to prize the diversity that enriches any nation,"[22]

> Brandwein, Paul F., *The Permanent Agenda of Man*

Integration has always been a key factor of the CRE-ACT approach. This aspect toward unification includes not only curricular materials, but the bringing together of students of varying ages, parents, professionals, and the community-at-large as well. Some such activities are preplanned and others just develop creatively and spontaneously as they evolve. Among the "constants" or"annuals" are:

The CRE-ACT Speech Festival

At this event, participants have the opportunity to learn to speak before an audience. Invitations are sent to public, parochial, private and home schools within an approximately fifty mile radius of the school. Students pre-school (four olds) through grade eight may register. Participants select a piece of literature or compose their own if they prefer, which they deliver three tines in the course of the day, each time before a different judge. Judges are chosen from the professional world, many from the local university. The festivities begin with a general assembly during which the participants are affirmed for their efforts to improve their communication skills and are encouraged to learn from and encourage one another. Three "rounds" follow. Participants change rooms for each round in order to be evaluated by different judges.

After results are tallied, an awards assembly is held. "Traveling" trophies and ribbons are awarded. All participants leave with a token of some kind for their efforts.

St. Nicholas Day

This is the day on which students use their creativity to make Christmas ornaments for their Christmas tree, their home, and gifts for others. (This activity has been described in the Religion Space.)

Liturgical Religious Services

These are held in relation to major religious feasts and vary according to options available. They may take place in a church, chapel, school building, or outside, depending on the nature of the observance. Students assist in planning for, preparing and carrying out these services. Their families and friends are invited to attend.

Thanksgiving Feast

On the day before Thanksgiving vacation, the staff and students prepare and serve a Thank You Luncheon to parents, senior citizen volunteers, benefactors, and anyone who has contributed to the welfare of the school in any way. Younger students design placemats and decorate the room; older students serve the food and provide entertainment.

Talent Show

At the time of the Christmas Party, children choose a form of sharing with others a talent or skill which they have developed outside of school. Surprises are in store as parents accompany their children on musical instruments, dance with them, tell and act out stories peculiar to their heritage, etc. Often skills and talents that no one outside the family knew about are shared and developed in new ways.

Depending on the cycle of the curriculum which is in focus during a specific school year, there may be a Renaissance Festival, A Planet Day, a State of Idaho Fair, Fairy Tale Adventures, Science Fair, etc. Activities of this nature help the students to become more aware of the talents of their classmates and the benefits that can be realized by combining their efforts. Parents and the community at large are better able to understand and realize that they are an integral part of the school and its efforts.

The All School Production

The feature for which CRE-ACT is best known is its annual All School Production. Each spring the school produces a full-length scripted play. Typically there are six performances. Three are held during the school day for students of other schools. For the public generally, two are scheduled for evenings and one for Saturday afternoon. The play is performed on a professional stage. All CRE-ACT students, four- year old preschoolers to sixth graders, perform in the play. In addition, students assist in the production by helping with costumes, props, and sets. The choice of the play is determined before the school year opens and in relation to the cyclic theme of the year. This arrangement makes it possible to integrate the setting (time and place), plot, pattern of development, interaction of characters etc. into the basic curriculum of that specific year. Some of the values experienced from this emphasis in the curriculum may be stated as follows:

1. Drama is the primary artistic medium in the CRE-ACT curriculum. The play gives students an opportunity to use the dramatic awareness and skills they have acquired during the year in a formal public setting.
2. The play challenges everyone from the most experienced teacher to the youngest student. The faculty is not made up of theatre professionals. Students observe their teachers modeling the same behavior which is expected of them in class each day, struggling with unfamiliar problems, trying and refining solutions. They consult and problem solve together— How should we build the Cyclop's cave? How build a raft for Huck and Jim? How should a character who has to make a quick change backstage be dressed?
3. The play provides a common goal that requires close collaboration from everyone.
4. Students develop the ability to act as part of a team and work through the inevitable tensions and conflicts that arise as part of the process. The fulfillment felt at the end, following the verification of a job well done, is very much a shared experience.
5. Elementary school children get to do something that matters. Children work as hard at producing a good play as their parents do at doing their work well, and their motive for doing so is intrinsic.
6. The play is produced by and for everyone, not just the talented actors in the student body. All are required to stretch their talents to the limit. Many, because they are shy or lack self-confidence, find that they are capable of performing better than they ever thought possible.

7. The play provides different vehicles for learning and expression. Students experience a variety of learning processes and modalities. Some students have first learned to read by memorizing their dialogue. This is a natural way for students to make the connection between written language, spoken dialogue, and physical expression and actions.

For most students, the annual production stands out as one of the most fulfilling experiences of their lives. Many have traveled great distances to return and witness "A CRE-ACT play." A list of the productions from 1978 when this aspect of the curriculum began follows.

1978—The Velveteen Rabbit
1979—Alice in Wonderland
1980—The Wizard of Oz
1981—Pinocchio
1982—Snow White
1983—Charlotte's Web
1984—The Hobbit
1985—The Lion, the Witch, and the Wardrobe
1986—A Wrinkle in Time
1987—Wind in the Willows
1988—Mrs. Frisby and the Rats of Nihm
1989—Peter Pan
1990—Alice in Wonderland
1991—The Jungle Book
1992—Tom Sawyer
1993—A Connecticut Yankee in King Arthur's Court
1994—Swiss Family Robinson
1995—The Ballad of Robinhood
1996—The Hobbit
1997—Snow White
1998—Huckleberry Finn
1999—The Odyssey
2000—The Wizard of Oz
2001—American Myth, Legend, and Folklore
2002—A Pantheon of Heroes in Greek Mythology
2003—Charlotte's Web
2004—Mrs. Frisby and the Rats of Nihm
2005—The Glass Slipper
2006—The Jungle Book
2007—The Princess and the Pea

The advantages of an integrated curriculum which uses CREative ACTing as its medium are evident in all aspects of the students' lives. Nancy J. Legge of Idaho State University in Pocatello who observed many of the CRE-ACT productions and activities affirms: "The long term benefits of creative drama, like thinking on one's feet, problem solving, collaboration skills, a sense of presence, empathy, the ability to put creative ideas into action, are held up as essential qualities for success in the world. They are equally important in the board room, on the assembly line, and in the home."[23]

ADMINISTRATIVE AREAS

The Green Room

The Director's Space

> "Creating a curriculum is a beneficent but awesome task. One asks, 'What kind of a world do we want for children?' This is a terrible question, for it forces us to deal with the ideal. But nothing else is worth thinking about if we want to create an environment, a particular world, for children. And this world we seek is not chaotic. It allows both freedom and order; it has relevance; it has structure. It achieves unity—unity within diversity"[24]
>
> Paul Brandwein, *The Permanent Agenda of Man.*

This is the space in which the CRE-ACT concept is centered. It is the space in which new accents, pertinent extensions, fresh insights, and probable adaptations of the concept are explored—a space to dream dreams and to ask questions such as "What if . . . ?", "Why . . . ?", "and then. . . ?". This is the office of the Director, the person who upholds and interprets the pristine design of the playwright, the originator of the plan. The Director is aware of the pivotal points in the structure and what modifications it can support. Its blueprint is the script of the production. Everything begins with the script. The Director transfers the world of the play contained in the script to the concrete reality of the stage—the school.

The Green Room is the "holding space" where staff, students, parents and professionals are free to come for information, clarification, encouragement, or assistance in order to better relate to the school and its program.

The role of the Director is to bring the play and the audience—students, parents, faculty, and the community—together in performance. A Director encourages, supports and releases inner power of the actors and then observes performance. During performance the Director entrusts the actors to develop their roles and withholds comments. Periodically thereafter times for coming together are arranged so that the actor can obtain further assistance to develop and advance professionally, as well as to provide opportunity for suggesting creative alternatives to improve performance.

The Stage Manager

The Principal's Office

> "True leadership is the art of changing a group from what it is into what it ought to be."[25]

Virginia Allen, Lessons in Leadership

While the Director interprets the manner in which the CREative ACTing script is performed, the principal as Stage Manager becomes responsible for the condition of the physical space that will insure smooth operation of performance. The stage includes not only the classrooms and school premises proper, but also all places to which the school activities take students and staff. The Stage Manager is responsible for assembling and maintaining all of the elements on stage: i.e., structure and design of classroom settings, lighting operations, sound and communication systems, and properties necessary for quality performance.

At the time of production the Stage Manager becomes the representative of the Director, overseeing all involved in performance. Smooth operation requires that actors are "in character," entrances are made on time, cues are taken from one another, and movement proceeds on schedule. Absences, tardiness, personality conflicts, failure to comply with expectations, shortcomings of all kinds which are patterns of human interaction become the principal's concern. As often as is needed, the principal confers with the Director, instructors hold faculty meetings, students assemble for discussion, and all explore ways of enhancing the performance. Rehearsals may need to be reintroduced, but the performance continues and gains momentum. All these "centering" operations are organized and implemented in the principal's office of The Franciscan CRE-ACT School.

NOTES

1. McCarthy, Mary, The Women's Leadership Forum Advertising Brochure.

2. Editors of Read Magazine, "Words, Words,Words" *10 Plays and Choral Readings* (Middletown, Con.: Xerox Corporation (1965), 19.

3. Holmes, Oliver Wendel, *The Iron Gate And Other Poems* (Whitefish, Mont.: Kessinger Publishing, 2004). http:www.abebooks.com/servlet/Book DetailsPL?bi=841851618&s.

4. Editors of Read Magazine, "Words, Words, Words", 16.

5. Editors of Read Magazine,"The American Dream", 3.

6. Longfellow, Henry W., "A Psalm of Life", Quotations http://quotations about http://quotationa about.com/cs/poemlyrics/a/A Psalm of Life.htm (6 Oct. 2007) .

7. Heady, Eleanor B., Tales of Shoshoni Bannock Indians (Chicago: Follett Publishing, 1973), 13.

8. McLane, D. Frank, "Monsters of Mathematics", *Should have Been a Cowboy* (Self published with National Beta Club, 2003), 64.

9. McClane, *Should Have Been*, 98.

10. Theresa of Calcutta, Mother, bookmark.

11. Thoreau, Henry D., *Light From Many Lamps*, ed. Lillian Eichler, Motivational Quotes.com.:Search Results (May 17. 2007).

12. Dunne, Patsy, Unpublished Lesson Plans.

13. Boyer, Ernest J., For the Advancement of Teaching, (Unpublished).

14. Hall, Stanley, Quotations About Dance,http://cc.mnscache.com/cache.aspx ?q=72337425531748mkt=en=US&lng=en-us&lng=706d+60&formCPRE (18 Nov. 2007).

15. *Jump or Jiggle*, Poetry Anthology, Publication 06473, North Haven, CT.

16. Riley, Richard, Eloquent Evidence: Arts at the Core of Learning (Washington D.C.: National Endowment for the Arts, Oct. 1995), 7.

17. Benson, Pastor Bruce, St. Olaf College, Northfield, MN (Minnesota Public Radio: 20 March 2007).

18. Boyer-Alexander, Rene, Campbelle-Holman, Margaret; de Frece, Robert; Goodkin, Doug; Henderson, Betsy M.: Jothen, Michael; King, Carol; Miller, Nancy L.T.; Rawlins, Ivy , Share the Music, Grade 2 (New York, Macmillan/McGraw-Hill, 2003) 32-33.

19. Boyer-Alexander, Rene, Grade 1,

20. Wirth, Marien Straeswick, Verna Shotwell, Rita and Stemmler, Patricia, *Musical Games, Finger Plays, and Rhythmic Activities for Early Childhood* (West New York: Parker Publishing, 1983), 110, 209.

21. Fleschman, Paul, Joyful Noise (New York: Harper & Rowe, 1988), 11.

22. Brandwein, Paul, *The Permanent Agenda of Man* (New York: Harcourt, Brace, Jovanovich, 1971), 42.

23. Legge, Nancy J., Instructor's Notes, (Pocatello, Idaho, Unpublished).

24. Brandwein, *Permanent Agenda*, 6.

25. Allen, Virginia, The Women's Leadership Forum, Advertising Brochure.

Catching the butterfly

Becoming the butterfly—small group

Becoming the butterfly—class size

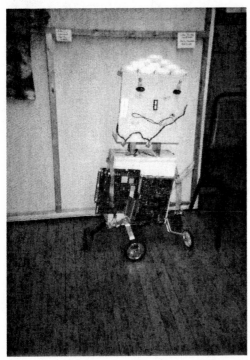

Inventing new machines that can walk and talk

Inventing new machines that can see

Egyptian mask

Let me introduce our heroes . . .

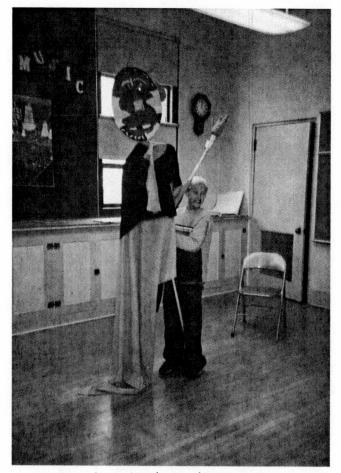

Let me introduce our heroes . . .

Historical Time Line—How will we be represented?

Historical Time Line—How will we be represented?

Historical Time Line—How will we be represented?

Rectangle with hands, triangles with arms and legs

Octagon with hands

Hexagon

Mathematical formulas bridge us with reality

Yarn designs of math shapes

Yarn designs of math shapes

Do straight lines become curves?

What will it be?

Chapter Ten

Curtain Call

"All students will value the fine arts and humanities as lifelong companions that enrich experience and enhance their understanding of individuals and society."[1]

State of Idaho Fine Arts Content Guide and Framework

APPRAISAL

Whenever there is an investment of energy, be it personal, political, social, industrial, etc., the question of value follows immediately. Was the effort worthwhile?

A major factor to be considered in evaluating a program is its controlling purpose. What does it attempt to accomplish? Then, what means and strategies are employed to achieve this end? Given the above, one should be able to ascertain the degree of effectiveness to which these measures achieve that purpose. This procedure should insure that criteria specific to the matter being assessed are used.

In assessing the CREative ACTing program, the controlling purpose to be kept in mind is the focus on personal development. The design for assessment therefore should include:

1. Ability to actively participate in a rapidly changing pluralistic society.
2. Development of skills intended to prepare the participant to be ready to face, relate to, and effectively order situations as they occur.
3. Creative exploration of new applications for basic facts and principles learned.

Such a design requires norms capable of maintaining their purpose, even if applied to changing situations. For this reason, both objective and subjective criteria are employed. Objective measures include appropriately chosen teacher- selected measurements, reports, and standardized tests of curricular materials. These criteria are objective and can be used for all students. They have a degree of constancy about them. Basic facts are an essential starting point. They are the raw material for creative ventures, the inspiration for artistic expression, and provide a firm basis on which to build. Facts are the matter from which new concepts are derived.

As a school approved by the State of Idaho, The Franciscan CRE-ACT School uses, but is not confined to exclusively, The Idaho State Achievement Test (ISAT). Curricular areas tested in this program include Reading, Language Arts, and Mathematics for grades 2-6. Participation in this program provides a basis for comparison on both National and State levels. In spring 2007, 87% of the students scored as basic, proficient, or advanced.

In addition to this standardized test, every other year students in grades 4-8 take the Direct Math and Direct Writing Assessments which are composed and evaluated by educators within the state of Idaho. In these tests students are evaluated on how well they understand and can apply specific skills and knowledge in these two areas.

The Idaho Reading Indicator (IRI) is a timed test administered to students in grades K through 4. This test indicates whether or not a student is reading on grade level, and in what areas a student may have difficulty. In Spring 2007, 85% of the students scored at or near grade level on the spring test.

Standardized tests assess mastery in terms of how well students perform in relation to others. They do not measure how well any of the students actually understand the subject, nor do they take into account any reasoning or problem solving procedures. Only the correct or incorrect answer to a question or problem is recorded and evaluated. In contrast, the Direct Assessments require that students set down on paper the process used to arrive at the "finished Project." CRE-ACT teachers value the Direct Assessment measures more than the Standardized Tests, although both are informative in their own way.

Subjective criteria are essential to a program like CRE-ACT. Many of the variables that enter in affect personal growth and development. In addition to individual uniqueness and opportunities (or lack of) for positive experiences, there are familial, political, and social influences. Furthermore, some achievements are "intangible" without a format suitable for representing them. In active learning and performance oriented activities, it may be others who benefit even more than the student. Subjective criteria used here include personal remarks of professionals, parents, anecdotal records, a survey conducted with former students, and awards received.

CRITIQUES

Educational Auspices

New York University
School of Education
Division of English Education, Speech, and Educational Theatre
829 Shimkin Hall
Washington Square
New York, NY 10003
Telephone: (212) 5980-2921, 2922, 2923

March 24, 1975

Sister Dorothy Prokes
583 W. Sexton Street
Blockfoot, Idaho 83221

Dear Sister Dorothy:

The faculty of the Program in Educational Theatre, The School of Education, Health, Nursing, and Arts Professions, New York University, has read with great interest a report of your activities in Idaho dealing with creative dramatics, child drama and educational theatre. The program in Creative Study (CRE-ACT), which you first developed with success in Wisconsin, continues to grow with impressive results. And, of course, your work in teacher training makes a great contribution to many schools throughout the state and beyond.

We remember with affection and admiration the excellence of your research undertaken as a doctoral candidate in this Program, and, so our new recruitment brochure demonstrates, take pride in the accomplishment of your excellent dissertation, "Exploring the Relationship Between Participation in Creative Dramatics and Development of the Imaginative Capacities of Gifted Junior High School Students." This thesis is cited frequently for its significance as a major experimental study in child drama.

We are convinced that the direction in which your work is moving qualifies your programs as among the most stimulating and innovative in the country. If at some future point it would be possible for our Program to join the efforts with yours, we would be most interested in pursuing ways we could be of mutual service.

The faculty here congratulates you upon the achievement of your various projects in Idaho, with the hopes that they will continue to prosper under your leadership.

Cordially,

Lowell Swortzell
Professor of Educational Theatre
Director, Program in Educational Theatre

Idaho State University
Pocatello, Idaho
College of Education

April 2, 1976

Dr. Dorothy Prokes, F.S.E.
Star Route, Box 170
Big Sky Road
Pocatello, Idaho 83201

Dear Dr. Prokes:

I have read your proposal for a private elementary school in Pocatello. The concept you have in the school is exciting, innovative, and, what's more, educationally sound.

For too long we have felt that one type of education could solve the problems for all children. Unfortunately, if this is true we have never been able to come up with that perfect type of education. Some children prosper under certain conditions and others need different kinds of humane treatment.

The foundation of your school is so personal, with small classes and individual attention coupled with creative acting that an educator cannot help but be impressed with the intent.

All of us prosper (whether involved in public or private education) when a sound program like what you propose is to be offered. The College of Education is willing to cooperate with you and your school in the placing of student teachers, or providing an opportunity for our pre-service education students a place to observe different methodologies. I am sure there will be some of our students who would like to work on small projects in your school and this could be arranged on a supervisory type of program.

I am painfully aware that with small classes and being a private school there will have to be tuition. I am sure that a number of those who can afford to pay these tuition charges for their children will be glad to do so. Parents want the best for their children. Unfortunately, not all parents can afford these tuition charges and so I hope that you are able to arrange some scholarships for students who can profit from your program.

We will look forward to seeing what we can do within the College to philosophically support your school and the goals inherent therein.

Sincerely,

Richard L. Willey, Dean

Mesa College
Grand Junction, Colorado 81501
School of Humanities and Fine Arts

January 29, 1979

Sister Dorothy Prokes, F.S.E., Ph. D.
Creative Acting
309 N. Garfield
P.O. Box 723
Pocatello, Idaho 83201

Dear Sister Prokes:

I have just finished my third "study" of the brochure you gave me on your work in *Creative Acting*. It is absolutely amazing. The imaginative and creative foresight on your part for the "whole" human experience is most humanitarian and spiritual elevating. The concept that imagination and creative enters most significantly into every aspect of the curriculum at the very beginning of a child's education is definitely an enriching and rewarding experience.

It appears to me that by your approach a child/student would be "freed" from any previous conceived or imposed limitations as to the potential experience a student may experience. Through this avenue of integrated curriculum approach, a child will find a more expressive self and a more adjusted and accepted individual to himself/herself as a unique part of creation.

It was my good fortune to have the "brief encounter" of the Creative Acting experience.

Sincerely,

Dan M. Showalter, Dean
School Humanities/Fine Arts

Albertson College of Idaho
Department of Theatre
Box #111/2112 Cleveland Boulevard
Phone/Fax/Message: (208) 459-5836

February 28, 1996

1996 Awards Committee
American Alliance for Theatre and Education

RE: 1996 Creative Drama Award

Dear Committee Members:

It is my pleasure to write in support of the nomination of Mother Dorothy Prokes for the 1996 AATE Creative Drama Award. I believe Dr. Prokes deserves the award in recognition of her development of the only elementary school core curriculum in the United States (known to child drama experts) based precisely on creative drama. As you may know, this creative drama-driven core curriculum is at the heart of every student's education at Cre-Act School in Pocatello, Idaho, the private school she founded and continues to operate as Principal.

A detailed portrait of Dr. Prokes philosophy and her creative drama-driven core curriculum appears in an article I published: "Creative Drama as Core Curriculum," *The Drama/Theatre Teacher*, 5:4 (Spring, 1994), pp. 7-12. You undoubtedly have the article, since the magazine comes with AATE membership, and so I hope you'll consider it part of this letter of nomination.

What you *cannot* see in the article is the faces of my creative drama students (almost all elementary or early childhood majors) when I take them over to Pocatello to sit in on creative drama sessions run by Dr. Prokes or by one of her faculty. The absolute wonder on the faces of my students, especially the older ones, when they *see* what she does and how she does it; the amazement in their voices when they talk about the 11-year olds they saw really excited about parts of speech (for example) and competing actively to be part of that learning experience. Now, admittedly, these college students are people quite devoted to elementary education, but nevertheless it looks to me as though exposure to the Cre-Act method is the most provocative and stimulating experience they have in their preparation for a teaching career. I seldom see so many faces so bright with excitement as in the van on the way back from Pocatello.

Therefore it is with great pleasure that I give my strongest support to the nomination of Mother Dorothy Prokes for the 1996 Creative Drama Award.

Cordially,

Dr. Charles R. Hannum, Chair
Department of Theatre

Parents of Students

"What I enjoy seeing at CRE-ACT is the community built around the teachers and children—with each contact of caring and constructive interest adding to the web of relationships. I would wish this for other children as well as my own."

Allison McDougall

"The Franciscan CRE-ACT School reaches attributes in children that other schools don't touch. The caring is real and the learning is real. The best part is not that I, as a parent, have learned so much about children and learning. The best part is that my children have a foundation for learning that will sustain them for their life times, and I have been able to share it with them. I am profoundly grateful."

Gretchen Vanek

I just wanted to drop you a line and tell you how the legacy of CRE-ACT is living on through Tim. He was in a play this summer called "Take Me Along", a musical comedy about life in the early 1900's in America. There were only 3 children in the play. The rest were adults. (Now) Tim is going to be Peter Cratchit in "A Christmas Carol" in the ACT Theatre in Seattle. An exciting part for him is that they are going to pay him $1,700 to do the play! The play runs from Nov. 26 to Dec.26, 12 shows a week. Tim is going to be busy . . . still happily acting."

Karen Quandt.

"My son Jake attended CRE-ACT from kindergarten through sixth grade. His experiences at CRE-ACT were at all times exceptional. The curriculum and vision of the school allowed him to meet his goals on all levels—educational, creative, and personal. CRE-ACT consistently exceeded my expectations for his educational experience. The skills he acquired at CRE-ACT are serving him well. He willingly accepts scholastic challenges, has time management skills, and has an excellent work ethic. I know he learned those skills and more at CRE-ACT School."

Virginia B. Allen, Ed.D., LPCP, NCC
Licensed Professional Counselor

"Your vision, relentless dedication, and tireless work have impacted the Pocatello community as a whole, and the CRE-ACT Community in particular. The many lives you have touched are forever enriched by your spirit.

Thank you for the gifts you have given to our children: the license to be independent thinkers; the will to be creative learners; the confidence to be public speakers; the strength to be role models; the desire to be good citizens; a strong sense of community.

Thank you for the greatest gift you could ever give to parents; the opportunity to be directly involved in our children's education. We are forever grateful to you for educating us, mind, body, and spirit."

Stacey, Kathy, and Hailey Rogers

Former Students

"CRE-ACT is the best school in the world. . . .I would like to go there for ever!"

Alexandria Nash

"The most valuable thing I have ever received came from CRE-ACT. Here I learned to think and work independently."

Maxie Rogers

"CRE-ACT is a safe place. You put your mind to things and do what you think!"

Emily Newhouse

"CRE-ACT has been my yellow brick road since the first day I started there. The skills taught in the classrooms (speech, acting, writing, cooperation and teamwork) have had much to do with how I live my life today.

Every student was encouraged to find a talent and use it to his/her full ability. Mine was speech. During the fall speech festivals I had an opportunity to uncover my abilities and work with them. This has worked to my advantage even today as I made a speech at a fundraising banquet for Heritage Christian School. I had the honor of speaking in front of 500 adults. Because of CRE-ACT philosophy I was able to write and read my speech with confidence. The school has helped prepare me for life and given me the ability to work with people and in front of people at a moment's notice. Had it not been for CRE-ACT, I would not be the same person I am today."

Christi Morgan.

Others

Idaho State Journal, March 29, 1984.
Responses from Audience Attending "The Hobbit."

"The Hobbit" is no longer a lonely man since the first presentation of the CRE-ACT School's annual show March 23rd. He now has a large following of adventurers who are looking forward to the next presentation slated tonight and Friday at 7:30 p.m. at Frazier Hall.

"Middle Earth will never be the same again after the CRE-ACT crew's interpretation of 'The Hobbit'," said one show-goer, pointing out that the show went well and a great deal of hard work was reflected.

Others described it thusly:

"CRE-ACT has accepted a very ambitious challenge in recreating the magical world of Middle Earth on stage and has pulled it off rather effectively".

"Appetizing. . . .effervescent. . . .exhilarating . . . inspiring . . . dramatic. . . .Gripping"

"Really great. I brought 17 Girl Scouts, and they all enjoyed it."

"Your production is a credit to the staff, students and parents of the CRE-ACT School. It is encouraging to see some really creative productions being done with children. I am impressed with the time and effort put into this production."

" Absolutely delightful and entertaining! The cast was expressive and communicated the message of challenge and adventure and how personal growth occurs through both."

AWARDS

The following awards were accorded to The Franciscan CRE-ACT School students and/or its administrator and founder:

2006

April

NASA Idaho Space Grant Consorrtium's art contest "Exploring Mars"

Stephen Pelletier, First Place, Grades K-3.
Naomi Behrend, Director's Choice, Grades K-3
Frances Slater, Honorable Mention, Grades K-3

1996

November

Artist in Service Award, Pocatello, Idaho; sponsored by SEICA

October

Member of People to People International Theatre group to tour National Republic of China

September

Recipient of Governor's Award for Support of Arts Education in Idaho.

August

Recipient of National Creative Drama Award at The American Alliance for Theatre and Education Convention, New York City.

1990

One of 20 administrators of schools invited to the National Beta Networking Conference in Baltimore, Maryland.

1985

April

Named "Outstanding Elementary School Principal" for 1985 by the John F. Kennedy Center for the Performing Arts.

1975

October

CRE-ACT was Idaho's representative to the National Conference for the Alliance for Arts in Education Conference at The J.F. Kennedy Center for The Performing Arts. It was one of six schools in the United States to receive a $1,000 grant to take a representative group of children to demonstrate the program. Thirteen students ranging from grades 2-8 made the trip.

January

State Delegate to the Conference for Talented/Gifted/Creative in Wichita, Kansas.

1972

April

Declared a University Honors Scholar by New York University

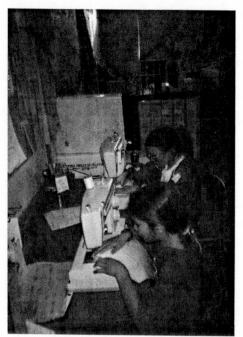

Students learn to use the sewing machine

Goose from "Swiss Family Robinson"

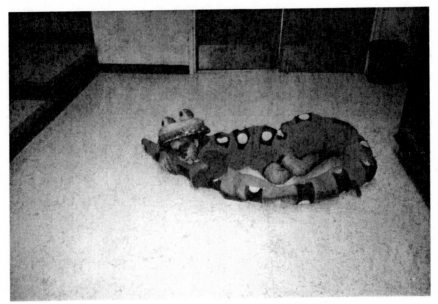

Boa constrictor from "Swiss Family Robinson"

Donkey from "Swiss Family Robinson"

Donkey from "Swiss Family Robinson"

Jackal and Goose from "Swiss Family Robinson"

Spider from "Charlotte's Web"

Wilbur from "Charlotte's Web"

Templeton and Wilbur from "Charlotte's Web"

Who am I?

Masks enhance many occasions

Drama, Lewis and Clark Expedition—Westward Movement

Section Four

IMPLICATIONS
FOR THE FUTURE

Chapter Eleven

The Sequel

"The future is not a result of choices among alternative paths offered by the present, but a place that is created—created first in the mind and will, created next in activity. The future is not some place we are going to, but one we are creating. The paths are not to be found, but made, and the activity of making them, changes both the maker and the destination."[1]

John Schoar

One of the most common concerns voiced today by anyone interested in education can be summed up in the word "reform." Reform, by its very nature involves change, and change immediately implies a struggle. What kinds of changes are needed and how should they be implemented? What knowledge, values, skills, and sensibilities should schools nurture in students in order to prepare them for these adjustments?

Contemporary educational changes involve a wide range of technological and computerized skills. A high percentage of a student's life is immersed in computer use, in game playing, in creating artificial environments, virtual people and relationships—a make-believe world. Controls have some how been "switched." Instead of acting as a person whose body is directed by live controls—the senses, intellect and will, capable of making choices and decisions—the student frequently employs a "mechanized tool" to create an artificial virtual world which somehow is given precedence, and in which one is expected to find a place. Diversity has difficulty conforming to uniformity.

The preceding pages confirm the fact that the concept of change has always been an integral part of the CRE-ACT approach. The principle agent of change is the student. The norms and principles of the students' formation are designed to prepare them to handle sustaining change. The CRE-ACT principles remain constant, regardless of the age or experience of the student. They are rooted in and built upon the basic nature of man and woman as human beings. This is where the stability of the program lies. It is the manner of incorporating these principles and adjusting them to the facts of real life situations that vary in time and place.

The provision of real life experiences provides means for students to become involved in the learning process in a way that gives them ownership. They recognize change in themselves, identifying characteristics they have in common with others, as well as those which identify themselves as unique. They "paint" their own self-becoming image, i.e., "paint their own wagon," and are motivated to "get on the way." Seeing "the other" (person, group, or situation) calling forth their individual unique potential gives them courage and confidence. Strength comes from knowing that they are not alone in this effort.

The best investment we as educators can make for the future is to equip students with a sound, stable system of values which respects life, truth, justice, beauty and faith. This will prepare them to meet and respond to real life situations—to improvise, to act, to live and become all they are intended to be. With quality preparation such as this, they will be able to interpret and follow the road map legend which will lead to their own personal fulfillment and that of others into the future. They will know

WHERE THEY ARE GOING!

NOTE

1. Schoar, John, Motivational Quotes.com: Search Results (17 May 2007).

Index